WHY MARRIAGE MATTERS

AMERICA, EQUALITY, AND GAY PEOPLE'S RIGHT TO MARRY

EVAN WOLFSON

Simon & Schuster

New York   London   Toronto   Sydney

SIMON & SCHUSTER
Rockefeller Center
1230 Avenue of the Americas
New York, NY 10020

SIMON & SCHUSTER and colophon are registered trademarks
of Simon & Schuster, Inc.

For information about special discounts for bulk purchases,
please contact Simon & Schuster Special Sales at
1-800-456-6798 or business@simonandschuster.com

Designed by Jeanette Olender

Manufactured in the United States of America

1   3   5   7   9   10   8   6   4   2

ISBN 0-7432-6458-4

To Dan Foley of Hawaii,

Mary Bonauto of GLAD, Jon Davidson of Lambda Legal,

Tim Sweeney of the Evelyn & Walter Haas Jr. Fund,

and my many other gay and non-gay friends and colleagues

in the lesbian and gay civil rights movement

ACKNOWLEDGMENTS

I would like to thank my friend and superb writing collaborator, Jon Barrett; my agent, Fred Morris; my editor, Rob Weisbach; and the team at Simon & Schuster for making the writing of my first book possible.

Many of the ideas and materials set forth in this book were shaped during the years I spent working at Lambda Legal Defense & Education Fund (Lambda Legal), America's preeminent national gay legal rights organization; partnering with wonderful advocacy groups such as Gay & Lesbian Advocates & Defenders (GLAD), the National Center for Lesbian Rights, and the American Civil Liberties Union's Lesbian/Gay Rights Project; and building a movement with diverse gay and non-gay groups and activists in Washington, D.C., and many states and countries.

Thanks also go to the staff, steering committee, and supporters of Freedom to Marry for helping me give time to this book project and for sharing the content we have developed for our Web site, www.freedomtomarry.org, the starting point for non-gay and gay people wanting to know more about "gay marriage."

And, as always, love and thanks to my parents, Joan and Jerry Wolfson, exemplars in love and marriage; to my sibs, Alison, David and Nancy, Michael and Jane; to my nie/phews, Emily, Ben, Charlie, and Simon; and to Cheng, who keeps me laughing.

CONTENTS

*Those who deny freedom to others deserve it not for them-
selves; and, under a just God, can not long retain it.*

Abraham Lincoln [1]

*A prime part of the history of our Constitution . . . is the
story of the extension of constitutional rights and protections
to people once ignored or excluded.*

U.S. Supreme Court Justice Ruth Bader Ginsburg (1996) [2]

*I don't think for a moment we thought we would have a
child that had fewer civil rights than we have had.*

Mimi Goodman, mother of a gay child (2004) [3]

*Because marriage is a basic human right and an individual
choice, the State should not interfere with same-gender couples who choose to marry and share fully and equally in the
rights, responsibilities, and commitment of civil marriage.*

The Marriage Resolution

CHAPTER ONE

WHAT IS MARRIAGE?

Civil marriage is at once a deeply personal commitment to another human being and a highly public celebration of the ideals of mutuality, companionship, intimacy, fidelity, and family.

Massachusetts Supreme Judicial Court,
Goodridge v. Department of Public Health (2003)[1]

How the world can change,
It can change like that,
Due to one little word:
"Married."

John Kander and Fred Ebb,
"Married," *Cabaret* (1966)

Depending on which linguistic expert you ask, there are anywhere from two thousand to seven thousand different languages spoken in the world today. That's a huge number to put your mind around—even for someone who lives in Manhattan, where seemingly hundreds of those languages can be heard on the subway on any given day. Still, I'm willing to bet that each of these languages has something in common with the others: a word that means marriage.

No matter what language people speak—from Arabic to Yiddish, from Chinook to Chinese—marriage is what we use to describe a specific relationship of love and dedication to another person. It is how we explain the families that are united because of that love. And it universally signifies a level of self-sacrifice and responsibility and a stage of life unlike any other.

Now of course, different cultures and times have had many different conceptions of marriage, different rules and different ways of regarding those who are married—not to mention different treatment for married men and married women. We will explore some of those differences in this book: differences in who can marry whom and when, in how to end a failed marriage (or if you even may), in how many people you can marry, in the involvement or noninvolvement of the state and religion, and in the consequences that come with being married. But with all this variety and all the changes that have occurred in marriage over time and in different places, including our country and within our lifetime, it is clear that marriage has been a defining institution in virtually every society throughout history. Given its variety and omnipresence, it is not surprising that when people talk about marriage, they often mean different things.

Consider all the different dimensions of marriage in the United States alone. First, marriage is a personal commitment and an important choice that belongs to couples in love. In fact, many people consider their choice of partner the most significant choice they will ever make. It is a relationship between people who are, hopefully, in love and an undertaking that most couples hope will endure.

Marriage is also a social statement, preeminently describing and defining a person's relationships and place in society. Marital status, along with what we do for a living, is often one of the first pieces of information we give to others about ourselves. It's so important, in fact, that most married people wear a symbol of their marriage on their hand.

Marriage is also a relationship between a couple and the government. Couples need the government's participation to get into and out of a marriage. Because it is a legal or "civil" institution, marriage is the legal gateway to a vast array of protections, responsibilities, and benefits—most of which cannot be replicated in any other way, no matter how much forethought you show or how much you are able to spend on attorneys' fees and assembling proxies and papers.

The tangible legal and economic protections and responsibilities that come with marriage include access to health care and medical decision making for your partner and your children; parenting and immigration rights; inheritance, taxation, Social Security, and other government benefits; rules for ending a relationship while protecting both parties; and the simple ability to pool resources to buy or transfer property without adverse tax treatment. In 1996, the federal government cataloged more than 1,049 ways in which married people are accorded special status under federal law; in a 2004 report, the General Accounting Office bumped up those federal effects of marriage to at least 1,138. Add in the state-level protections and the intangible as well as tangible privileges marriage brings in private life, and it's clear that the legal institution of marriage is one of the major safety nets in life, both in times of crisis and in day-to-day living.[2]

Marriage uniquely permits couples to travel and deal with others in business or across borders without playing a game of "now you're legally next of kin; now you're legally not." It is a known commodity; no matter how people in fact conduct their marriages, there is a clarity, security, and automatic level of respect and legal status when someone gets to say, "That's my husband" or "I love my wife."

Marriage has spiritual significance for many of us and familial significance for nearly all of us. Family members inquire when one is going to get married, often to the point of nagging. Many religions perform marriage ceremonies, many consider marriage holy or a sacrament within their faith, and the majority of American couples get married in a religious setting—although the percentage of those having a purely civil ceremony is at nearly 40 percent and growing. As far as the law is concerned, however, what counts is not what you do at the altar or whether you march down the aisle, but that you get a civil marriage license from the government and sign a legal document in the vestibule of the church, synagogue, temple, or mosque—or at city hall, a court, or a clerk's office. As a legal matter, what the priest, minister, rabbi, or other clergy member does is *witness* the couple's commitment and attest to their conformity with the requirements for a civil marriage license.

As ubiquitous and varied as the institution is, the word *marriage* and its myriad translations throughout the world also have a unique meaning that children often use in making a joke. Who doesn't remember taunting friends with a question like this: "If you love candy so much, why don't you marry it?" Of course we know

now—and I suppose we must have known then—that the punch line was in the question itself. The joke shows that though they may well "go together like a horse and carriage," *marriage* is different from *love*. *Love* is a word that can be applied to anything from your favorite song and your best-fitting pair of Levi's to your parents, your roommate, or your boyfriend, while *marriage* signifies an unequaled commitment. And, as the childhood taunt illustrates, that's a distinction most of us have understood since we were kids.

Still, marriage is now the vocabulary we use to talk of love, family, dedication, self-sacrifice, and stages of life. Marriage is a language of love, equality, and inclusion. While recognizing that marriage should not be the sole criterion for benefits and support—nor the only family form worthy of respect—most of us take marriage seriously and most of us do marry.

None of this is to say that marriage is the right choice for everybody. One need only meet a happy single or divorced person to know that many people are pleased with their decision to avoid matrimony. And, of course, we've all been to weddings where we wonder how *she* could marry *him*. As splendid as the institution is in the abstract, and as revered as marriage is in virtually every society, one need only look at the divorce rate to know that there are bad marriages and marriages that, without fault, have ceased to work.

There is clearly a difference between *marriage* and *marriages,* between the institution and the choices and conduct of real couples in their commitment. For better or for worse, marriage is about choice, whether it be the choice to "make it official" with your beloved and to accept the protections and the responsibilities that accompany that decision; the choice to work at your marriage and make it rewarding and good; the choice to betray or divorce a spouse; or the choice to avoid the institution of marriage altogether.

But marriage hasn't always been about choice. In fact, as we will see later, it has historically been a battlefield, the site of collisions within and between governments and religions over who should regulate it. But marriage has weathered centuries of skirmishes and change. It has evolved from an institution that was imposed on some people and denied to others, to the loving union of companionship, commitment, and caring between equal partners that we think of today.[3]

In ancient Rome, for example, a man was not considered a citizen until he was married, and in many countries today, people, no matter how old, live under the roof, and remain under the control, of their parents until they wed—often a powerful incentive to marry (and a far cry from our idea of marriage as a choice made out of love). And you might be surprised to learn that, for example, the Catholic Church had nothing to do with marriage during the church's first one thousand years; marriage was not yet recognized officially as a Catholic sacrament, nor were weddings then performed in churches. Rather, marriage was understood as a dynastic or property arrangement for families and the basic social unit, *households* (then often extended families or kin, often including servants and even slaves). Family life and law in past centuries, let alone marriage, were very different from anything we'd recognize in the United States today.

Battles over marriage have taken place in America, too. As we'll talk about more in later chapters, there was a time when our country excluded African-Americans from marriage altogether, prohibited people from marrying a partner of the "wrong" race, denied married people the use of contraception, and stripped women of their rights and even personhood—essentially making them chattel—at the altar. It took decades and decades of fighting to change these injustices. And change still needs to take place in the hearts of many, not to mention the law. As recently as 1998 in South Carolina and 2000 in Alabama, 40 percent of the voters in each state voted to keep offensive language barring interracial marriage in their respective state constitutions.

But fortunately, the general story of our country is movement toward inclusion and equality. The majority of Americans are fair. They realize that exclusionary conceptions of marriage fly in the face of our national commitment to freedom as well as the personal commitment made by loving couples. Americans have been ready again and again to make the changes needed to ensure that the institution of marriage reflects the values of love, inclusion, interdependence, and support.

Such a change came about as recently as 1987, when a group of Americans who had been denied the freedom to marry came before the U.S. Supreme Court. Before the justices issued an opinion in the case, *Turner v. Safley*, they had to determine what role marriage plays in American society. Or, more precisely, what role marriage plays in American law.

After careful consideration, the justices outlined four "important attributes" of marriage: First, they said, marriage represents an opportunity to make a public statement of commitment and love to another person, and an opportunity to receive public support for that commitment. Second, the justices said, marriage has for many people an important spiritual or religious dimension. Third, marriage offers the prospect of physical "consummation," which of course most of us call something else. And fourth, the justices said, marriage in the United States is the unique and indispensable gateway, the "precondition," for a vast array of protections, responsibilities, and benefits—public and private, tangible and intangible, legal and economic—that have real importance for real people.

The Supreme Court of course understood, as we discussed above, that marriage has other purposes and aspects in the religious sphere, in business, and in people's personal lives. The justices knew, for example, that for many people, marriage is also important as a structure in which they can have and raise children. But when examined with the U.S. Constitution in mind, these four attributes or interests identified by the Court are the ones that have the legal weight. And after weighing these attributes, the justices ruled—in a unanimous decision—that marriage is such an important choice that it may not be arbitrarily denied by the government. Accordingly, they ordered that the government stop refusing marriage licenses to the group of Americans who had brought the case.

That group of Americans was prisoners.

Seventeen years after the Supreme Court recognized that the choice to marry is so important that it cannot be arbitrarily denied to convicted felons, one group of Americans is still denied the freedom to marry. No matter how long they have been together as a couple, no matter how committed and loving their relationship, and no matter how much they need the basic tools and support that come with marriage, lesbian and gay Americans in this country are excluded from the legal right to obtain a civil marriage license and marry the person they love.

Who are these same-sex couples and how does the exclusion from marriage harm them and their families?

They include Maureen Kilian and Cindy Meneghin of Butler, New Jersey, a committed couple ever since they met more than thirty years ago during their junior year in high school. Maureen works part-time as a parish administrator for Christ Church in nearby Pompton Lakes, where her job includes entering the names of married couples into the church registry. Cindy, meanwhile, is the director of Web services at Montclair State University. The women wish that one of them could stay at home full-time to help care for their two children, Josh and Sarah. But because they aren't married, neither of them is eligible for family health insurance through her employer, so both of them have to leave the kids in order to stay insured.

"We are good citizens, we pay our taxes, and we are caring parents—but we don't have the same equality as other Americans," Maureen told the *New York Times.* "We're tired of having to explain our relationship. When you say you're married, everyone understands that." More than anything, Maureen and Cindy told the *Times,* they want spousal inheritance rights, so that if one of them dies, the other one can stay in their home without having to pay crippling estate taxes to the Internal Revenue Service. That security comes with marriage.[4]

Alicia Heath-Toby and Saundra Toby-Heath also live in New Jersey and have been a couple for more than fifteen years. Alicia is a deacon and Saundra an usher in the Liberation in Truth Unity Fellowship Church, an African-American congregation, and they regularly participate in church cookouts, picnics, dances, and family activities as well as services. The women have children and grandchildren, bought a home together in Newark, and pay taxes. When Alicia had surgery, Saundra took weeks off from her work as a FedEx dispatcher to take care of her. Denied access to family health insurance and required to pay two deductibles instead of one because they are not married, Saundra and Alicia want to enter a legal commitment to match the religious one they already celebrated in their church.

"If two complete strangers met each other last week and got legally married today, they would have more rights under the law than our relationship has after fifteen years of being together. That's not fair," Saundra and Alicia told their lawyers at Lambda Legal Defense & Education Fund. "We pay first-class taxes, but we're treated like second-class citizens."[5] They worry about their kids and each other, and they want the best legal and economic protection they can get for their family. That protection comes with marriage.

Tony Eitnier and Thomas Arnold have been life partners for more than ten years, but until recently they faced every day with the fear that it would be their last together. That's because Tony is from the United States and Thomas is from Germany. Unlike most of America's close allies, such as Canada and the United Kingdom, our country discriminates with policies that do not allow gay citizens to remain together with committed partners from other countries under the family unification principles that normally apply in immigration. "It [is] a mental battle not to go crazy, never knowing if your partner is going to have to leave tomorrow," Tony told the Associated Press. "You become paranoid." [6]

Because Germany is one of more than fifteen countries with an immigration policy that treats binational same-sex couples equally, Tony and Thomas moved to Berlin, where they can live together without fear of a forced separation. That's little comfort for Tony's family in San Diego, California, though. "I'm very close to my family, and it was extremely traumatic to have to leave," Tony said. "My parents are bitter at the government." [7] The couple holds on to the hope that they can return to the U.S. and live openly and legally as a couple in Tony's own country, America, the land of the free. That right comes with marriage.

Chris Lodewyks and Craig Hutchison of Pompton Lakes, New Jersey, have been committed partners since they met when they were freshmen in college, more than thirty years ago. As is the case for many middle-aged couples, Chris and Craig have spent a good part of the past decade looking after their aging parents. When Chris's mom was battling cancer at the end of her life, Craig took time off from work to help care for her. And now that Chris is retired, he can spend time helping Craig's elderly mother. The men also are active in the community. Chris has spearheaded a town cleanup day, with businesses donating prizes to hundreds of volunteers, and Craig serves on the board of a YMCA camp. "Gay and lesbian topics are in the news every day," Chris told New Jersey's *Bergen County Record.* "This is an emotional time, and some people may be looking at this like it's going too fast. But it's not going too fast. It's time for us to have the same civil rights as everyone else." [8]

Chris and Craig have shown the personal commitment to each other, have done the work, and have undertaken on their own many of the family responsibilities of a married couple, including caring for each other's parents. Now they want the full legal responsibilities and protections that the government bestows on married couples. "After thirty years of commitment and responsibility the government treats our accomplishments together as worthless," Craig said. [9] Full protections and legal responsibility come with marriage.

Julie and Hillary Goodridge of Jamaica Plain, Massachusetts, have been in a committed relationship for sixteen years and are raising a young daughter together. One day the women played the Beatles song "All You Need Is Love" for their daughter, Annie, who was five years old at the time. When Hillary asked Annie if she knew any people who loved each other, Annie named several of her mothers' married friends. "What about Mommy and Ma?" Hillary asked. "Well," Annie replied, "if you loved each other you'd get married." At that point, Hillary later told *Newsweek* magazine, "My heart just dropped." [10]

It wasn't the first time that the freedom to marry would have helped clarify the Goodridges' family relationship for the people around them. The most dramatic illustration of how exclusion from marriage harms their family took place after Julie's caesarean delivery of Annie, when Hillary was denied entry into the ICU to see her newborn daughter. "They said, 'Only immediate family,' and I had a fit," Hillary told *People* magazine. [11]

Who wouldn't have a fit? And who should have to go through an ordeal like that, especially at such an important, trying, and hopefully joyous time as the birth of a child? The Goodridges want assurance that they won't encounter similar obstacles the next time

Julie, Hillary, or Annie is hospitalized or in need. That assurance comes with marriage.

In fact, exclusion from the freedom to marry unfairly punishes committed same-sex couples and their families by depriving them of critical assistance, security, and obligations in virtually every area of life, including, yes, even death and taxes:

◆ Death: If a couple is not married and one partner dies, the other partner is not entitled to get bereavement leave from work, to file wrongful death claims, to draw the Social Security payments of the deceased partner, or to automatically inherit a shared home, assets, or personal items in the absence of a will.

◆ Debts: Unmarried partners do not generally have responsibility for each other's debt.

◆ Divorce: Unmarried couples do not have access to the courts or to the legal and financial guidelines in times of breakup, including rules for how to handle shared property, child support, and alimony, or to protect the weaker party and the kids.

◆ Family leave: Unmarried couples are often not covered by laws and policies that permit people to take medical leave to care for a sick spouse or for the kids.

◆ Health: Unlike spouses, unmarried partners are usually not considered next of kin for the purposes of hospital visitation and emergency medical decisions. In addition, they can't cover their families on their health plans without paying taxes on the coverage, nor are they eligible for Medicare and Medicaid coverage.

◆ Housing: Denied marriage, couples of lesser means are not recognized as a family and thus can be denied or disfavored in their applications for public housing.

◆ Immigration: U.S. residency and family unification are not available to an unmarried partner from another country.

◆ Inheritance: Unmarried surviving partners do not automatically inherit property should their loved one die without a will, nor do they get legal protection for inheritance rights such as elective share or to bypass the hassles and expenses of probate court.

◆ Insurance: Unmarried partners can't always sign up for joint home and auto insurance. In addition, many employers don't cover domestic partners or their biological or nonbiological children in their health insurance plans.

◆ Parenting: Unmarried couples are denied the automatic right to joint parenting, joint adoption, joint foster care, and visitation for nonbiological parents. In addition, the children of unmarried couples are denied the guarantee of child support and an automatic legal relationship to both parents, and are sometimes sent a wrongheaded but real negative message about their own status and family.

◆ Portability: Unlike marriages, which are honored in all states and countries, domestic partnerships and other alternative mechanisms only exist in a few states and countries, are not given any legal acknowledgment in most, and leave families without the clarity and security of knowing what their legal status and rights will be.

◆ Privilege: Unmarried couples are not shielded against having to testify against each other in judicial proceedings, and are also usually denied the coverage in crime-victims counseling and protection programs afforded married couples.

◆ Property: Unmarried couples are excluded from special rules that permit married couples to buy and own property together under favorable terms, rules that protect married couples in their shared homes, and rules regarding the distribution of property in the event of death or divorce.

◆ Retirement: In addition to being denied access to shared or spousal benefits through Social Security as well as coverage under Medicare and other programs, unmarried couples are denied withdrawal rights and protective tax treatment given to spouses with regard to IRAs and other retirement plans.

◆ Taxes: Unmarried couples cannot file joint tax returns and are excluded from tax benefits and claims specific to marriage. In addition, they are denied the right to transfer property to each other and pool the family's resources without adverse tax consequences.

And, again, virtually all of these critical, concrete legal incidents of marriage cannot be arranged by shelling out money for an attorney or writing up private agreements, even if the couple has lots of forethought to discuss all the issues in advance and then a bunch of extra cash to throw at lawyers.

It's not just same-sex couples who are harmed by society's refusal to respect their personal commitment and human desire for the protections and statement of marriage. Going back to that juvenile quip, "If you love it, why don't you marry it," let me tell you one of my earliest memories of when I realized I was gay.

I am lucky to have a very close and loving family, and grew up living with my parents, sister, and two brothers. One night—I couldn't have been more than eleven or twelve—my mother and I were watching something on TV and talking. Dad was out on his weekly bowling night and the other kids must have already gone off to sleep. I remember saying to my mom, in what must have seemed an out-of-the-blue declaration, "I don't think I'll get married." I don't remember if, or how, my mom responded. But I do remember that I realized I might be excluded from the joys of married life, and felt there was something in the picture society showed me that I didn't fit into, before I could tell my mom or even fully understand that I was gay.

Many gay kids, even before they hear the word *gay* and associate it with themselves, and even before they fully understand how their own lives will take shape, do understand that they are different from their friends. For the most part, of course, gay kids grow up in the non-gay world—raised by non-gay parents; surrounded by mostly non-gay siblings, friends, relatives, and teachers; exposed to non-gay images and expectations everywhere, from church, television, and popular music. And yet, until now our society has also sent those kids the message that the dream of romantic love, of commitment, of family, of marriage is not for them. America tells its children that the dream of "first comes love, then comes marriage" is not for you if you're gay.

This is wrong and has to change.

Unlike the members of most other minority groups, we gay people are not usually born into our own identity or community, or into families that share or understand our sense of self; we have to find our way largely on our own, often after working through negative messages about homosexuality, or a lack of understanding from family members, peers, churches, and the other institutions that people rely on for self-identification, solidarity, and support.

When I told my mother I didn't think I'd get married, I was not rejecting marriage; I was working out my own sense of difference in a world that said I could not have what marriage signifies— life as a couple with the person you choose, legal recognition, acceptance—given the restrictions placed both on marriage and on people like me.

Again, I was lucky. I never doubted that my parents loved me and would love me, even if and when they found out I was gay. That doesn't mean it was easy for my parents. When, years later, I told them I am gay, it meant there were some differences in the life they imagined for me, differences they in turn had to accept as part of their unconditional love for me.

Even with loving parents and personal self-confidence, as a young child not even knowing the word *gay*, I was led to believe that I had to reject a pattern of life that didn't seem to be available for me with the kind of partner I could truly love, someone of the same sex. In a childish way, I thought it was "marriage" I didn't fit into, when, in fact, the love and commitment marriage signifies were perfectly appropriate dreams for me. It was exclusion, rejection, and the denial of the freedom to marry that were and are unnecessary, harsh, harmful, and wrong.

Notice here that I'm not using terms like "gay marriage" or "same-sex marriage." That's because these terms imply that same-sex couples are asking for rights and privileges that married couples do not have, or for rights that are something lesser or different than what non-gay couples have. In fact, we don't want "gay marriage," we want marriage—the same freedom to marry, with the same duties, dignity, security, and expression of love and equality as our non-gay brothers and sisters have.

Gay people have the same mix of reasons for wanting the freedom to marry as non-gay people: emotional and economic, practical and personal, social and spiritual. The inequities and the legal and cultural second-class status that exclusion from marriage reinforces affect all gay people, but the denial of marriage's safety net falls hardest on the poor, the less educated, and the otherwise vulnerable. And the denial of the freedom to marry undermines young gay people's sense of self and their dreams of a life together with a partner.

Of course our country needs to find ways other than marriage to support and welcome all kids, all families, and all communities.

Marriage is not, need not, and should not be the only means of protecting oneself and a loving partner or family. But like other Americans, same-sex couples need the responsibilities and support marriage offers legally and economically to families dealing with parenting, property, Social Security, finances, and the like, especially in times of crisis, health emergency, divorce, and death. And gay people, like all human beings, love and want to declare love, want inclusion in the community and the equal choices and possibilities that belong to us all as Americans.

Marriage equality is the precondition for these rights, these protections, this inclusion, this full citizenship. The freedom to marry is important in building strong families and strong communities. What sense does it make to deny that freedom to Maureen and Cindy, Alicia and Saundra, Tony and Thomas, Chris and Craig, or Julie and Hillary?

How many more young people have to grow up believing that they are alone, that they are not welcome, that they are unequal and second-class, that their society does not value their love or expect them to find permanence and commitment?

How many non-gay parents and family members have to worry or feel pain for their gay loved ones? What mother doesn't want the best for all her kids, or want to be able to dance at her lesbian daughter's wedding just as she did at her other child's?

As Americans have done so many times in the past, it's time we learn from our mistakes and acknowledge that lesbian and gay Americans—like people the world around—speak the vocabulary of marriage, live the personal commitment of marriage, do the hard work of marriage, and share the responsibilities we associate with marriage. It's time to allow them the same freedom every other American has—the freedom to marry.

Chapter Two

Why Now?

People talk about the white backlash . . . Now, my answer to this question is that there is really no white backlash, because that gives the impression that the nation had decided it was going to solve this problem and then there was a step back because of developments in the civil rights movement. Now, the fact is that America has been backlashing on the civil rights question for centuries now . . . The backlash is merely the surfacing of prejudices, of hostilities, of hatreds and fears that already existed and they are just now starting to open.

Martin Luther King Jr.[1]

I am neither politician nor legal expert . . . But my daughter and her Afro-Brazilian husband couldn't have married thirty-five years ago, so I see this as a Rosa Parks moment for marriage equality. Millions of same-sex couples in this country should no longer have to sit in the back of the marriage bus. I'm just a mom who years ago learned to be comfortable about same-sex couples, a mom who wants all her children to have equal rights to marry, and wants this for other same-sex couples too. Today, I'm a mom happy that my son and his beloved have gotten married.

Ann Davidson, a mother in San José, California (2004)[2]

In 1996, as is the case now, America was in the midst of an intense national discussion over gay people and the freedom to marry. As I'll describe a little later in this chapter, then, as now, Congress and state legislatures were considering measures aimed at deepening discrimination against the then-prospective marriages of same-sex couples. Non-gay Americans began to wrestle, most in good faith, with conflicting feelings about traditions, fairness, and what is familiar. Americans began to rethink how our society treats its gay sons and daughters.

One of those non-gay Americans was Congressman Sonny Bono, ex-husband of Cher and father of Chastity Bono. A California Republican, Representative Bono described his struggle over what he recognized was ultimately not a legal issue, not the Constitution's guarantee of equality, not the harm posed by or to gay people, or much of what was being said in support of the anti-gay measure pending before Congress . . . but rather, his own discomfort. In an unusually personal, convoluted, yet extraordinarily revealing exchange with openly gay Congressman Barney Frank before the House Judiciary Committee, Bono admitted his inability to embrace change and equality at that moment, and his inability to justify the failure to do so:

> [I]t's clear to me, Mr. Chairman, that . . . my job here is to try to interpret the Constitution and then act on that interpretation, representing the people. . . . Barney's a good friend of mine. And I see his point of view, and I appreciate his fight. He's fighting as hard as he can because he's a human being; he has

these feelings; he's gay; my daughter's gay. He has to live this way. . . . [But] I think we go beyond the Constitution here. I think we go beyond these brilliant interpretations here, and I think we have hit feelings, and we've hit what people can handle and what they can't handle, and it's that simple . . . I don't love my daughter any less because she's gay, and I don't dislike Barney any more because he's gay. . . . [M]y response back to [Barney] is, you're absolutely right, but the other side of it is this has taken people to as far as they can go, and then no justifiers— I don't want to justify it because I can't. You just go as far as you can go, and then that's why I want to say to you again, honestly, I can't go this far as you deserve even. . . . [3]

Before responding with several powerful substantive arguments, Frank thanked Bono for his "candor and the decency that motivates it." And Barney Frank, too, concluded his part of the exchange with a personal plea: "[L]et us be like anyone else . . . no one is asking you to do anything else, and if it bothers people, turn your head, but don't inflict legal disabilities that carry out that feeling." [4] But in 1996, Sonny Bono just wasn't ready, America wasn't ready, and the discrimination deepened.

Now here we are as a nation today, and the discussion continues. As in 1996, while opponents pursue their own political agendas, many people of good will are truly struggling. Today in fact, it seems you can't turn on the television or open a newspaper or magazine without finding a story that has something to do with gay people and marriage. CNN, Fox News, Univision, MTV, *Time* magazine, the *New York Times, Atlanta Journal-Constitution, Bozeman Daily Chronicle, Pittsburgh Post-Gazette,* even *Brides* magazine— there isn't a news outlet that isn't talking about people grappling over whether or not to end marriage discrimination against same-sex couples.

If you are just tuning in to the discussion, or are uncomfortable with it, or if it is not your major concern, it is understandable that at times, like Sonny Bono in 1996, you might not wish to hear about it. But as this civil rights movement of gay couples and non-gay allies advances, as attacks on gay families continue state by state, as candidates are asked to declare their positions, and as right-wing groups press to amend the Constitution for the first time in its history to take away rights from a group of Americans, it is clear that the question of marriage equality is not going away.

I believe that it is the job of people like me—indeed, the job of all of us as fellow citizens and fellow human beings—to take objections and discomfort seriously. Talking things through—giving each other arguments, time, space, and a presumption of reason and good faith—is a necessary step to push past discomfort. Martin Luther King Jr. famously remarked that "I am not afraid of . . . tension, [for like] a boil that can never be cured so long as it is covered up but must be opened with all its ugliness to the natural medicines of air and light, injustice must be exposed, with all the tension its exposure creates, to the light of human conscience and the air of national opinion before it can be cured."[5] Or as Isaiah Berlin put it somewhat more delicately, "There is no pearl without some irritation in the oyster."

I, too, trust that once fair-minded people see the real stakes and real people involved; hear the stories and voices of the couples and kids harmed by the exclusion from marriage; think through the arguments made by both sides and measure them against realities, not hypotheticals; and accept that sometimes America must embrace change to end a wrong, then together we can move past the discrimination we might not have understood or undone in the past, and fulfill our country's commitment to equality under the law. Having had the benefit of more time, and having given more thought now than either the late Congressman Bono or the majority of Americans had in 1996, most people will want to do better than acquiesce in legal discrimination because of personal discomfort. Most Americans are ready to see committed couples and kids get the equality that all human beings, as Sonny Bono put it, "deserve."

It is good that the majority are indeed ready to be fair, and it is imperative that we redouble our conversations, for look at the cascade of important events that have made headlines just since June 2003:

+ Canada's three most populous provinces—Ontario, British Columbia, and Quebec—open the doors of marriage, removing discriminatory barriers. Thousands of same-sex couples, including thousands of American couples, have married in Canada, honeymooning on the welcoming side of Niagara Falls.

+ Hundreds of small, medium, and large newspapers all around the U.S. begin publishing announcements of gay people's weddings and commitment ceremonies, letting Americans everywhere see just how many gay people are in fact living in committed partnerships.[6]

+ In *Lawrence v. Texas,* a 6–3 decision written by a Reagan appointee, the U.S. Supreme Court holds that the Constitution provides deep protection for decisions regarding family, intimacy, love, and, yes, sex—and that gay people share equally in the right to make these important personal, life-defining decisions. Even dissenting Justice Antonin Scalia concedes that the Court's language and logic leave "on pretty shaky grounds state laws limiting marriage to opposite-sex couples."[7]

+ California passes an "all-but-marriage" law granting committed gay couples many of the rights and responsibilities afforded married heterosexual couples.

◆ A bipartisan national poll reports that 50 percent of registered voters support, or at least could live with, the government's granting civil marriage licenses to gay and lesbian couples with the same rights, responsibilities, and protections enjoyed by other married couples, as long as religious institutions do not have to recognize or perform these marriages.[8] A variety of polls almost daily show that the country is roughly divided in thirds: one third fully embracing same-sex couples' freedom to marry; another third strongly opposed not just to marriage equality, but to gay people or homosexuality, period; and a middle third not yet fully supportive but *ready* to respect the personal commitment of couples and reject discrimination.

◆ The Vatican calls on Catholic lawmakers to oppose legislation extending marriage rights to same-sex couples, and proceeds to condemn the use of contraception. The church throws immense financial resources into political battles in states such as Massachusetts and, in alignment with right-wing groups, promotes amendments to the U.S. and Massachusetts constitutions.

◆ President George W. Bush uses his State of the Union address to threaten to support such an unprecedented federal constitutional amendment and later formally endorses it as he kicks off his 2004 reelection campaign. "Our nation must defend the sanctity of marriage," Bush says (more on the amendment later).[9] The NAACP (America's oldest and preeminent civil rights organization), the National Hispanic Leadership Agenda (a broad and diverse coalition of Latino organizations and leaders), and the Leadership Conference on Civil Rights (the umbrella coalition of more than 180 civil rights groups) all denounce this assault on the Constitution and gay families. They are joined by both Democrats and Republicans, including many conservatives such as columnist George Will, Senator John McCain, and even former Congressman Bob Barr, who sponsored the so-called "Defense of Marriage Act" attacking gay people's freedom to marry, the discriminatory federal measure Sonny Bono was agonizing over in 1996.

◆ In November 2003, the Massachusetts Supreme Judicial Court rules that discrimination in marriage violates the state constitution, putting Massachusetts on the path to become the first state in the U.S. to grant same-sex couples marriage licenses. The constitutional command of equality is clear, the court holds, and the government simply does not have a good reason for excluding gay Americans from marriage. Responding to delaying tactics by state legislators, the court reiterates in February 2004 that marriage—not separate or barely established new mechanisms such as civil unions—is the only avenue to full equality.

◆ San Francisco Mayor Gavin Newsom orders city clerk Mabel Teng to begin issuing marriage licenses to same-sex couples. Phyllis Lyon and Del Martin, partners for fifty-one years, become the first same-sex couple to get married in the city. Thousands of other couples line up. Americans begin to hear the voices of the real people affected by marriage discrimination— same-sex couples and their kids. One *New York Times* article, for example, quotes several of the children whose parents had just gotten married:

> "It was so cool," said Gabriel, thirteen, who served as the ringbearer, after standing in line overnight with his parents. "I always accepted that 'Yeah, they're my moms,' but they were actually getting married. I felt thick inside with happiness. Just thick."

"Before it was, 'Oh, your parents are just partners,' " said
Max Blachman, the thirteen-year-old son of lesbian parents in Berkeley. "Now, they're spouses. So it's a bigger
way of thinking about them."
Speaking of his mothers' marriage, [eleven-year-old] Alex said:
"It is something I always wanted. I've always been around
people saying, 'Oh, my parents' anniversary is this week.' It's
always been the sight of two parents, married, with rings.
And knowing I'd probably never experience it ever. . . . Politically and officially, everybody now knows it's true—
they're together," Alex said of his moms. "It's something I
felt I needed to experience. I think people who think it's terrible have no heart whatsoever." [10]

◆ Other cities and counties follow in ending discriminatory restrictions; clergy and others speak out in support of
these families and weddings; and across America, nearly ten
thousand same-sex couples are married by the end of March
2004.

No wonder we're hearing so much about gay people and marriage.
America is again in a civil rights moment—and while courts and
legislatures grapple with how and when to end discrimination,
more and more people, gay and non-gay, are reexamining where
they stand and are speaking out. The country is moving closer
to ending marriage discrimination—much like Canada, Europe,
South Africa, and other leading U.S. allies—and Americans are
now fully engaged in an important discussion of how the denial of
marriage harms families while helping no one.

* * *

What is the history that led us to this civil rights moment?

Three years after the U.S. Supreme Court decided in 1987 that even convicted felons could not be arbitrarily denied the freedom to marry, three same-sex couples in Hawaii went down to the clerk's office to apply for marriage licenses. And when the clerk turned them away, these committed couples took their own case to court, generating unprecedented worldwide attention to the question: "What reason is there for continuing to deny gay couples marriage rights?"

If you're like most Americans, the Hawaii debate was very likely the first time you heard the words *gay* and *marriage* in the same sentence. And regardless of whether your reaction upon hearing these words was one of enthusiasm, indifference, discomfort, or concern, it's also likely that this was the first time you gave much thought to how the exclusion from marriage harms families or whether the government even has a good reason for saying no to committed couples who want to say, "I do."

Same-sex couples had challenged the exclusion before. As far back as 1971, for example, the Minnesota Supreme Court had blocked Richard John Baker and James Michael McConnell from legally tying the knot, and there were other couples denied marriage in Kentucky and Washington state. But those cases came at the dawn of the gay civil rights movement, before America had had a chance to realize that gay families are found in every county, gay people in every profession, gay individuals in nearly everyone's family, workplace, or social circle. This first wave of marriage cases came before the AIDS epidemic, which, as Frank Rich wrote in a brilliant 2004 *New York Times* piece, "in retrospect, made same-sex marriage inevitable. Americans watched as gay men were turned away at their partners' hospital rooms and denied basic rights granted to heterosexual couples coping with a spouse's terminal illness and death."[11]

By 1990, Americans had begun to see gay people as fellow human beings, connected to others, and hearts and minds began to open. As a result, when the Hawaii case came along, it launched an ongoing national discussion and produced worldwide momentum. As we've witnessed in the past few months, this has put "marriage and gays" on everyone's radar screen.

This chapter in our national civil rights debate started with three love stories.

Ninia Baehr and Genora Dancel met each other in 1990, when Ninia's mother, who worked with Genora at Honolulu's public TV station, introduced them. "I was just totally smitten," Ninia later told the *San Francisco Chronicle.* "Two weeks later I told my mom that I just had this feeling I'm going to be with this woman for the rest of our lives." [12] Three months later, Genora proposed to Ninia, who said yes.

The couple applied for a marriage license in December 1990 because, in love, they wanted the official recognition that comes with marriage. Genora and Ninia also wanted to be able to list each other on their respective insurance policies, but always felt the financial benefits marriage would provide them were secondary to the legal status and statement of commitment. "For me it was an emotional decision," Ninia told the *San Francisco Examiner.* "I had wanted a relationship for a long time, one that would last a long time. So when it finally happened, I wanted recognition of that." [13]

Joe Melillo and Pat Lagon met at a disco-dance lesson in 1978 and, much like Ninia and Genora, immediately fell in step with each other. "It was love at first sight," Joe later told the *Philadelphia Inquirer.* "For me, it was just the right person and the right time." [14] As they built a life together, they went into business with each other, opening a T-shirt printing company. After fifteen years as a committed couple, Joe and Pat wanted to go down the aisle and exchange vows. "When you're born Catholic, it's bred into you that you will meet someone, fall in love, and get married." Pat told the *Los Angeles Times*. "And that's the way we wanted it to be." [15]

Antoinette Pregil's daughter, Leina'ala, was four years old in 1981, when Antoinette met Tammy Rodrigues and the two women started dating. Soon Toni and Tammy were living together as a couple and Tammy became a new mother and the breadwinner for a new family. Unlike other breadwinners, though, she couldn't extend her work benefits to her partner or her child because she and Toni were not legally married.

Ninia and Genora's love, Joe and Pat's commitment to each other as a couple, and Antoinette and Tammy's concern for their child—the mix of reasons these couples, like so many others, had for wanting to get married—didn't count in the state of Hawaii. The clerk, upon advice from the attorney general, denied the requests for marriage licenses.

At this point the Hawaii couples first approached me to ask if I would be their lawyer, given my long-standing advocacy for the freedom to marry, even when many people in the gay equality movement, and most of the organizations, were not talking about it. At the time I worked at Lambda Legal, the nation's preeminent gay legal rights group. Contrary to the right-wing myth of a "gay agenda," Lambda and other movement organizations, as well as allies such as the American Civil Liberties Union, were divided internally over whether to challenge marriage discrimination. Because of these divisions, I was not allowed to take the case. That turned out to be one of the luckiest days in our civil rights history because it brought the couples and local activists to Dan Foley.

In 1990, Dan Foley was a well-known and respected civil rights attorney in a small Honolulu firm, having previously served as legal director of Hawaii's ACLU affiliate. Heterosexual, married, and the very involved father of two great kids, Dan was nevertheless no stranger to the kinds of discrimination gay people face. While with the ACLU he helped pass a Honolulu ordinance banning discrimination based on sexual orientation, sued to prevent a government official from denying the Miss Gay Molokai Pageant a permit because of prejudice that the pageant might cause the spread of HIV, and challenged nursing homes in Hawaii to admit people with AIDS as patients.[16]

Dan, who wrote his senior thesis in college on the treatment of sexual minorities in America, was no stranger to gay issues on a personal level, either. When young, Dan, like many non-gay kids, had gone through a phase of thinking he disliked gay people and homosexuality. His eyes and heart opened when he learned that a beloved uncle was gay. Dan had come to understand that difference should not mean disdain. So when local activists guided Ninia and Genora, Joe and Pat, and Toni and Tammy to Dan to ask if he would represent them in court, he didn't hesitate. "My first reaction was that it would be arrogant to deny [gay people] a right I have," Dan Foley later told the *Advocate* when the magazine named him one of the "25 Coolest Straight People."[17]

While many on the right attacked Dan for advocating marriage equality, few doubted that he was one of the state's top constitutional lawyers, a point Governor Ben Cayetano emphasized in 2000 when, after the historic marriage case had ended, he appointed Dan as a judge on the Hawaii Intermediate Court of Appeals. "His stand on legal issues, regardless of whether politically popular or not, speaks volumes of the courage and commitment he will bring" to the court, Cayetano said.[18]

Dan Foley is one of my personal heroes—for his integrity, wisdom, compassion, dedication, and skill, and because he exemplifies the crucial role that non-gay people can and must play in ending discrimination against gay Americans, discrimination unworthy of our country. Dan welcomed me as cocounsel on the case, and, by the end of our work together, I had a new non-gay brother.

Initially, in 1991, a lower court dismissed the couples' lawsuit. But on appeal, the Hawaii Supreme Court ruled on May 5, 1993, that the officials were violating the state constitution's guarantee of equal protection by prohibiting gay people from getting married. Justice Steven H. Levinson wrote in the majority opinion that "marriage is a basic civil right" and that Hawaii's exclusion "denies same-sex couples access to the marital status and its concomitant rights and benefits." [19]

While groundbreaking, the ruling in *Baehr v. Lewin* did not strike down Hawaii's marriage law, nor did it order the state to issue marriage licenses to the three couples or any other gay or lesbian couples in the state. Instead, the court held that if the state was going to discriminate against gay couples when it came to marriage, it had to show a "compelling state interest" for doing so. In other words, if government can't show a good reason for discriminating, it has to stop doing it. Put up or shut up.

For gay people—who since the 1971 court case in Minnesota had almost grown accustomed to judges and government officials rubber-stamping their second-class citizenship, including the denial of marriage—this decision in Hawaii was the first glimpse at an equality most of them had never imagined was possible. Representatives from national and local gay groups began meeting on a regular basis to enhance efforts to achieve the freedom to marry. And, for the first time ever, all the national gay organizations—from the National Gay and Lesbian Task Force on the left to the Log Cabin Republicans on the right—came together around a single statement of belief, the Marriage Resolution, which read:

Because marriage is a basic human right and an individual choice, the State should not interfere with same-gender couples who choose to marry and share fully and equally in the rights, responsibilities, and commitment of civil marriage.

Eager couples, energized activists, and non-gay allies all around the country began circulating this Marriage Resolution to ever-widening circles, asking people to begin a conversation about why the exclusion from marriage should end. The discussion spread from the law courts to the food courts, and non-gay Americans began to hear stories from real-life couples talking about their kids, their medical emergencies, their concerns about providing for their loved ones in the event of death or illness, and their dreams of having a legal commitment to match their personal commitment to the one they love. For the first time, people had to think about the impact of being denied marriage and whether there is a good reason to continue this discrimination.

And, as you might imagine, the Hawaii Supreme Court's decision did not escape the attention of gay rights opponents. They did not want a national discussion that might invite Americans to really see gay people as human beings harmed by assaults on, and the lack of protections for, their families and lives. These fierce opponents of gay people—who had been pushing anti-gay measures since the 1950s, and mounting a "culture war" campaign of anti-gay ballot initiatives from the 1970s on—launched an escalated attack almost immediately, trying to shut the discussion down.

The hallmarks of their attack were the classics trotted out in every civil rights chapter of American history: criticism of the courts for doing their job, claims that children are threatened, dehumanizing characterizations of gay people as animalistic and a threat to others, efforts to polarize people on religious grounds, and gloom-

and-doom assertions that marriage and civilization itself would crumble if a disfavored minority were allowed equal participation in the opportunities of society.[20] As the Hawaii debate progressed, the anti-gay groups became more and more active, and more organized. They saw the anti-gay attack as serving their larger anti-choice, anti–civil rights, anti-separation-of-church-and-state, ante-diluvian agenda.

In February 1996 (not coincidentally, a presidential election year), organizations such as Pat Robertson's Christian Coalition, Concerned Women for America, Colorado for Family Values—all of these, with Focus on the Family, Traditional Values Coalition, and the Family Research Council, the usual suspects then and now in orchestrated anti-gay attacks—held a press conference in Iowa. On the eve of the presidential caucuses, they announced their so-called "Campaign to Protect Marriage"; pushed a "marriage protection pledge" on the Republican Party's eventual presidential nominee, Bob Dole, and other candidates; and declared a well-funded effort to go state by state and to pressure the federal government into enacting anti-gay, anti-family, anti-marriage measures (including so-called "Defense of Marriage Acts," bills to further discriminate against the prospective legal marriages of same-sex couples).

Donald Kaul of Iowa's *Des Moines Register* wrote later:

> The single low point in the recently departed traveling medicine show known as the presidential-nominating process was the anti-gay rally staged in the name of The National Campaign to Protect Marriage. Bad enough they had the rally at all, but to see the men who would be president come one-by-one to suck up to the hateful demagogues who make up the leadership of the "pro-family" movement was revolting.[21]

In Hawaii, Mike Gabbard, then president of Stop Promoting Homosexuality America, claimed that allowing gay people to marry would undermine the American family. "I think that the whole issue of same-sex marriage comes down to examining the values of family, and society has an interest in keeping families strong. The bedrock of family is marriage," he said, adding a dash of the "homosexuality as sin" rhetoric. "They want homosexual behavior to be accepted on par with heterosexual behavior." [22]

On CNN's *Crossfire*, cohost Pat Buchanan fulminated against the "unnatural" idea of marriage equality: "Marriage between a man and a woman is a natural and hallowed institution, and to elevate a homosexual relationship, which is immoral, to that level represents the sanctioning and legalizing of a moral lie." [23]

And Robert Knight, then at the Washington, D.C.–based Family Research Council, blasted gay families' "counterfeit marriages," and made a familiar "slippery slope" argument. Extending the freedom to marry, he said, would "lead to calls for other relationships to be recognized, because if feelings are the key to recognizing a marriage, there's no logical reason why three or four people who say, 'We sincerely love each other,' should be denied this status." [24]

Knight was challenged on the premise of his diversionary argument—the false claim that marriage has always been the same and now people like me are trying to "redefine" it, which will lead to chaos and disaster—when he and I were interviewed by Ted Koppel on ABC's *Nightline* in 1995:

ROBERT KNIGHT: You know, this is an institution that has been universal, it's been backed by every major religion on the planet. It's the foundational building block of civilization, Confucius said 3,500 years ago. You can't mess with the formula and not do any damage to society.

TED KOPPEL: Oh, we've been messing with the formula for thousands of years. The formula is constantly being changed. You cannot argue, Mr. Knight, that the institution of marriage today bears any resemblance to the institution of marriage, for example, during the medieval days.

ROBERT KNIGHT: Yes, I can, and marriage has been pretty much the same over the centuries. Webster's dictionary defines it as the uniting of a man and a woman . . .

TED KOPPEL: In those days the unity between a man and a woman gave the man total rights over the woman, total dominion over the woman. It doesn't bear any resemblance at all to the kind of marriage that we have today.

ROBERT KNIGHT: Well, Ted, you still haven't taken an entire gender out of the equation. Marriage is the uniting of the two sexes. That's the definition. So when homosexuals say, "We want the right to marry," they've already got it, but they don't meet the requirements.

TED KOPPEL: Defined by whom? Defined by whom? Requirements as defined by whom?

ROBERT KNIGHT: Every major culture on the planet, all major religions. I mean, Ted, come on. I mean, you're—you're talking as if marriage hadn't existed, something we invented to oppress homosexuals, and that's nonsense.

TED KOPPEL: What I'm doing, Mr. Knight—and forgive me, we should let our other guest have a chance to get in here, too—but what I'm saying is that marriage—you refer to marriage as though it were some unchanging institution that has not, in any manner, been modified over the years, and clearly it has.[25]

As harsh and even silly as the opponents' assertions were, they didn't fall on deaf ears. Many politicians took their threats, false histories, and caricatures of who gay people are and what we want, and turned marriage equality into a political wedge issue. While the plaintiff couples in Hawaii waited patiently to see if the state would allow them to legalize their commitment to each other, legislators around the country succumbed to the organized anti-gay campaign, introducing bills that codified tacit restrictions on marriage and prohibited basic legal respect for same-sex couples' marriages performed in any other states, should any other state ever make them legal. Some of the measures even rolled back or denied what little legal protections—health coverage at work, bereavement leave—gay people had achieved piecemeal over decades. By the end of 2003, when gay people still remained second-class citizens unable to marry in any state in the country, the right-wing campaign had piled on additional layers of discrimination in a wave of laws adopted in more than three-fourths of the states, including, significantly, Hawaii.

These attack measures passed despite some of the most passionate testimony ever made in favor of equal rights. Consider the address Iowa state Representative Ed Fallon made to his colleagues as they debated one such anti-marriage bill in 1996. A non-gay man, Fallon was shocked at the level of prejudice that was leading his fellow legislators to rush to write discrimination into law. He stood on the floor and declared:

> I have anguished over this bill, not because there is any doubt in my mind as to how I should vote, but because I believe strongly that what we are dealing with here is the defining civil rights issue of this decade. . . . Back in the 1950s, many, many Americans were victimized by relentless, fear-driving red-baiting. There was a Bolshevik lurking in every bathroom, and you never knew but your neighbor or even your uncle might

turn out to be a communist. In the 1990s, red-baiting is out. But pink-baiting is in. Gay-bashing, generally thought of as a Friday night frolic for inebriated thugs, has its parallel expressions in voting booths, city council halls, and legislative chambers across this country. Today we are witnessing one of those expressions in the form of this bill. By singling out gay and lesbian marriages as a union unacceptable in the eyes of the law, we fuel the fires of ignorance, intolerance, and hatred. . . . [26]

Like Congressman Bono, Fallon described his personal journey as a non-gay man grappling with his own discomfort with gay people, and his evolving understanding of them:

Though I've never hated homosexuals, I used to fear them. When I was a kid growing up, the worst name you could call someone was a gay loser. And the stereotype that still pervades the minds of many in this chamber—that of the highly aggressive, promiscuous gay man seeking countless anonymous relationships—is the stereotype that I grew up with, and the stereotype that contributes to volumes of ignorance and volumes of fear. Over time, I've come to learn that this stereotype, like most stereotypes, is based on hearsay, not fact. The rogues who may fit the previous description are the exception to the rule, just as there are male heterosexual rogues who are aggressive, promiscuous, and constantly hitting on and harassing women. In my evolving experience with homosexuals, familiarity has displaced ignorance and dispelled fear.

I now count as friends and constituents many same-sex couples. Some have children. Most are in long-term, stable relationships. All are very decent, kind, and normal people. I make no effort to judge the integrity of what they do in their bedroom, and to their credit, they've never judged the integrity of what I do in mine. One lesbian couple I count as friends have two children the same age as my son and daughter. They attend the same elementary school as my children. They play together. They go to the same birthday parties. They swap overnights. These two children are healthy, bright, and courteous, and their parents probably do a better job of parenting than I do. Though you may have personal, religious reasons why this arrangement seems distasteful to you, there is absolutely no way you could rationally argue that this is not a stable, happy, healthy family. . . .

And Ed Fallon concluded by pushing past the personal to principle, in an acknowledgment that sometimes change is needed to break with discrimination and fulfill America's commitment to equality and opportunity for all:

> Ladies and gentlemen, this is not a marriage-protection bill. It is emphatically an anti-marriage bill. . . . What are you trying to protect heterosexual marriages from? There isn't a limited amount of love in Iowa. It isn't a non-renewable resource. If Amy and Barbara or Mike or Steve love each other, it doesn't mean that John and Mary can't. Marriage licenses aren't distributed on a first-come, first-serve basis here in Iowa. Heterosexual couples don't have to rush out and claim marriage licenses now, before they are all snatched up by gay and lesbian couples. Heterosexual unions are and will continue to be predominant, regardless of what gay and lesbian couples do. To suggest that homosexual couples in any way, shape, or form threaten to undermine the stability of heterosexual unions is patently absurd. And I know, you'll say: "What about the gay agenda?" Well, just as there turned out to be no Bolsheviks in the bathroom back in

the 1950s, there is no gay agenda in the 1990s. There is, however, a strong, well-funded, anti-gay agenda, and we have an example of its efforts before us today. . . .

If you are weighing the political consequences of opposing this bill and find they are too heavy, I'd like you to think about the great moral changes that have occurred in this country over the past 200 years. Ask yourself when you would have felt safe to speak in favor of the separation of the colonies from Great Britain? When would you have taken a public stand for the abolition of slavery? When would you have spoken in favor of women's suffrage? In the 1960s, when would you have joined Martin Luther King and others in calling for equal rights for African-Americans? When would you have spoken out against restrictive marriage laws banning interracial marriages? While the choice before us today . . . is a difficult one to make, it is nowhere near as difficult or dangerous as the choices faced by the many freedom fighters who came before us.

Legislators ignored heartfelt testimony from people like Joan Callahan, a fifty-year-old lesbian mother and philosophy professor with breast cancer, who took time from her chemotherapy treatment to explain to Kentucky lawmakers why the anti-marriage bill they were considering put her family at a disadvantage:

I shall address [you] under, if you will, two hats. The first is the hat that identifies me [as an employee of] the flagship university of this Commonwealth to work with students and to research and write on questions of ethics and public policy. The second hat identifies me in a very different way: as the partner of Jennifer Crossen and coparent of David Crossen, who are here with me before you today.

Let me tip my first hat. . . . I am one of the virtual handful of women at the University of Kentucky who hold the rank of full professor. I assume that this is sufficient to establish that my academic colleagues and our university administrators believe that I am not only competent to teach and write in my areas of study; but that my work is sufficiently outstanding to justify my placement among the university's highest-ranked teacher-scholars.

That said, what I have to say under my professional hat is brief and it is this: There simply is no credible secular argument for the claim that intimacy, including physical intimacy, between persons of the same sex is morally wrong. Period. End of story . . .

Let me finish under my other hat—the one I wear as a woman in a life relationship and as a mother. I indicate to you my life partner, Jennifer Crossen. I trust you will agree that she certainly appears to be a wholesome, healthy, and robust woman. I assure you that she is all of these things. And that is lucky for us. . . . As a self-employed person, she must purchase her and David's health care coverage independently. It would cost us more than three times as much to purchase for Jennifer and David the coverage I could purchase for them through my job if I were a man—a privilege my heterosexual colleagues are given systematically and without a second thought. It is lucky for us that I am facing cancer rather than Jennifer. Had she been the one of us with this disease, getting treatment for her on her insurance that she could otherwise get on my insurance would completely devastate us financially. . . .

Nor can I purchase health care for David through my job. And that is just not fair to David. I came into this child's life in 1988 when he was a year and a half old. I have fully parented him since then, sharing completely the economic and social responsibilities of a second parent. I am the only second parent he knows. . . . He knows me as the parent who has, as long as he can recall, been there helping him through everything from learning to swim, to learning to ride a bike, to learning to read and write, through learning to use power tools. . . .

I am Jennifer's spouse of over nine years now. I know that. And she knows that. And our families and friends know that. I am David's parent for all of his conscious life. I will always be his other mother. I know that. And David knows that. Yet, some who are here today would have you believe that we do not have family values. Shame on them.[27]

As we saw at the beginning of this chapter, the orchestrated attacks against the promise of marriage equality in Hawaii didn't stop at the state level. In the final months of the 1996 presidential campaign, the anti-gay effort made its way to Washington, where, following exchanges such as those between Representatives Bono and Frank, Congress overwhelmingly passed and President Clinton signed the so-called "Defense of Marriage Act," often referred to as "DOMA." This anti-marriage law excluded gay couples' lawful marriages—once the couples can actually get married—from all federal protections, responsibilities, and benefits that ordinarily accompany any other marriage in America. DOMA also claimed for the federal government the power to give states permission to ignore the lawful marriages performed in other states, a departure from how the states have always treated marriages celebrated in other states throughout American history, as we'll discuss more in chapter 8.

As many equal rights advocates had done in state legislatures across the country, U.S. Senator Chuck Robb of Virginia, one of fourteen senators who voted against the bill, explained his opposition in a moving fashion:

As one who represents a traditionally conservative state . . . many of my friends and supporters have urged me to sit this one out because of the political fallout, but I can't do that. I feel very strongly that this legislation is fundamentally wrong. Despite its name, [DOMA] does not defend marriage against some imminent, crippling effect. Although we have made huge strides in the struggle against discrimination based on gender, race, and religion, it is more difficult to see beyond our differences regarding sexual orientation. The fact that our hearts don't speak in the same way is not cause or justification to discriminate.[28]

And civil rights hero John Lewis, a Democrat from Georgia, was equally eloquent before the House of Representatives:

This bill is a slap in the face of the Declaration of Independence. It denies gay men and women the right to liberty and the pursuit of happiness. . . . Dr. Martin Luther King, Jr., used to say when people talked about interracial marriage, and I quote, "Races do not fall in love and get married. Individuals fall in love and get married." I have known racism. I have known bigotry. This bill stinks of the same fear, hatred, and intolerance. It should not be called the Defense of Marriage Act. It should be called the defense of mean-spirited bigots act. . . . Every word, every purpose, every message is wrong. It is not the right thing to do, to divide America.[29]

Keep in mind that DOMA, which really should be called the "Discrimination in Marriage Act," did not ban gay couples from marrying. What it did was intrude the federal government into marriage law for the first time, departing from centuries of American history in which marriage and family relations have been largely left to the states to regulate. Even more shockingly, DOMA created a caste system of first-class and second-class marriages, based on whose marriages the federal government likes or dislikes.

Opponents of equality hoped that DOMA and their well-funded campaign to enact similar discrimination state by state would shut down the discussion that was causing people to rethink the exclusion of gay couples from marriage. But on September 10, 1996, the same day the U.S. Senate followed the House of Representatives by passing the bill and sending it to President Clinton's desk—and nearly six years after the six plaintiffs in Hawaii applied for marriage licenses—Judge Kevin Chang opened his Honolulu court to hear the world's first full-fledged trial on gay people's freedom to marry. Dan Foley and I were there, representing the three couples.

From the opening day it was apparent that the state had failed to come up with any better reason than those of anti-gay activists Gabbard, Buchanan, and Knight for blocking same-sex couples from legal marriage. Three years after they were ordered to present a "compelling state reason" for the ban, the best the state attorney general's office could come up with was this: "All things being equal, a child is best parented by its biological parents living in a single household."[30]

Put aside for a moment that, as the U.S. Supreme Court said in the prisoners' case in 1987, people marry for many reasons, not all or even most of them related to children.[31] Put aside, too, that Hawaii was not denying marriage licenses to couples who don't have children. (This also, ironically, describes Pat Buchanan and his wife, Shelley, and Bob and Elizabeth Dole.) Put aside for now the clear reality that there are many family forms in America, and that kids are being raised by adoptive parents, nonbiological parents, single parents, and parents in blended families. Put aside the evidence that the kids being raised by gay parents are just as happy, healthy, and well adjusted as the children of non-gay parents. We'll talk about all of that more in chapters 4 and 5.

Even put aside, for now, the fact that out of the many family configurations, the only couples denied marriage licenses by our governments are same-sex couples, who are excluded from the freedom to marry across the board, in all circumstances, whether or not they are parents and whether or not they have kids who need support.

With all of that put aside, the biggest problem with the state's "compelling reason" for discrimination was this: Even if you accept its premise that non-gay parents are "better," it makes no sense to punish kids who have the "wrong" kind of parents by denying their families the benefits of marriage. As the *New York Times* later reported, during our cross-examination "the state's witnesses acknowledged that it would help the children of same-sex couples if their parents could wed. They agreed, too, that gay couples could be as competent at parenting as heterosexual ones."[32] The testimony of the state's own experts, as well as the evidence introduced by Dan Foley and me in our part of the case, completely undercut the idea that it is okay to deny committed gay couples (and gay parents) marriage licenses, because, the evidence showed, denial of marriage and its protections in fact harms, not helps, kids.

On December 3, 1996, in a historic decision, Judge Chang reviewed all the evidence, expert testimony, and arguments, and made the following legal findings, stating:

* The sexual orientation of parents is not in and of itself an indicator of the overall adjustment and development of children.
* Gay and lesbian parents and same-sex couples have the potential to raise children that are happy, healthy, and well-adjusted.
* Gay and lesbian parents and same-sex couples can provide

children with a nurturing relationship and a nurturing environment which is conducive to the development of happy, healthy, and well-adjusted children.

♦ Gay and lesbian parents and same-sex couples can be as fit and loving parents as non-gay men and women and different-sex couples.

♦ In Hawaii, and elsewhere, same-sex couples can, and do, have successful, loving, and committed relationships.

Based on these and other findings, the court concluded that the state "had failed to establish a causal link between allowing same-sex marriage and adverse effects upon the optimal development of children . . . [and] has not proved that allowing same-sex marriage will probably result in significant differences in the development or outcomes of children raised by gay or lesbian parents and same-sex couples, as compared to children raised by different-sex couples or biological parents."

"Simply put," Judge Chang wrote as he ordered the state to stop blocking gay people's freedom to marry, the state failed to present

sufficient credible evidence that demonstrates that the public interest in the well-being of children and families, or the optimal development of children would be adversely affected by same-sex marriage. Nor has [the state] demonstrated how same-sex marriage would adversely affect the public fisc, the state interest in assuring recognition of Hawaii marriages in other states, the institution of marriage, or any other important public or governmental interest.[33]

Thus, in the only full-fledged trial so far on gay people's freedom to marry, the evidence exposed as unsupported every argument used by the opposition both in and out of court. Gay and lesbian couples do have loving, successful, and, yes, committed relationships. Those relationships don't threaten heterosexual marriages or "traditional families." Gay and lesbian couples are just as good at parenting as their non-gay brothers and sisters. And, most importantly, their role as parents, their ability to care for their children, and the well-being of their kids are only *strengthened* when they have the freedom to marry.

* * *

And that brings us back to everything we're hearing about gay couples and marriage today. In the eight years since Judge Chang's ruling, more judges—like other good people wrestling with the question of why this discrimination should continue—are looking at the evidence, listening to the arguments on both sides, and coming to the same conclusion. That was the case in Canada, where, since June 10, 2003, courts in the three most populous provinces have ordered that marriage licenses be made available to committed couples.

That was also the case in Vermont in 2000, when five Republican appointees on the state supreme court heard a lawsuit brought by three same-sex couples seeking marriage licenses. Upon weighing all the evidence, and the insufficient justifications by the state for the discrimination, the justices declared that the state legislature must extend all the benefits of marriage to these and other same-sex couples, who, they said, "seek nothing more, or less, than legal protection and security for their avowed commitment to an intimate and human relationship." This the court added, "is simply, when all is said and done, a recognition of our common humanity."[34] The decision in *Baker v. Vermont* led to the state's first-of-its-kind civil-union law, intended to provide committed same-sex Vermont couples with state-level benefits and obligations parallel to those af-forded married non-gay couples (discussed in chapter 7).

And that was the case in Massachusetts, where on November 18, 2003, the Supreme Judicial Court ruled that under the state consti-tution, same-sex couples share an equal freedom to marry. "Mar-riage is a vital social institution," Chief Justice Margaret Marshall wrote in *Goodridge v. Department of Public Health*. "The exclusive commitment of two individuals to each other nurtures love and mutual support. It brings stability to our society." [35] The denial of marriage to gay couples harms families and helps no one the court concluded.

So once again, as in 1996, our country finds itself in a heated dis-cussion about the freedom to marry and gay Americans. Just as the decisions in Canada, Vermont, and—most prominently now—Massachusetts are bringing the nation closer than ever to marriage equality, opponents are pulling out the big guns (and the big wal-lets) and trying to turn marriage into a political wedge. Since, as described, they already failed to shut down this discussion by pass-ing the federal "denial of marriage" law along with dozens of other anti-gay measures in the states, this time around they have taken aim at the U.S. Constitution itself. They are pushing a constitu-tional amendment that would tie the hands of all states and all fu-ture generations, preventing them from providing marriage equality and other family protections to gay people and even, believe it or not, unmarried heterosexuals.

I love history, and eagerly devour books and programs about our country and its civil rights struggles for equality and inclusion. Where some get jazzed by heartwarming personal anecdotes and *People* magazine–type stories (not that there is anything wrong with that), my friends tease me that my reading list tends to alternate be-tween books about Lincoln and Hitler.

Well, Hawaii underscored an important historical lesson, and so, beginning in 1996 at that trial, I began carrying two pieces of paper in my wallet. The first was Congressman John Lewis's speech against the federal anti-marriage law, quoted earlier. The second was this passage from another civil rights hero, Frederick Douglass:

> If there is no struggle, there is no progress. Those who profess to favor freedom and yet deprecate agitation are people who want crops without plowing the ground. They want rain without thunder and lightning. . . . Power concedes nothing without a demand. It never did and it never will. People might not get all they work for in this world, but they certainly must work for all they get.[36]

Following Judge Chang's civil rights ruling in Hawaii, opponents from around the country poured millions of dollars into Hawaii and successfully lobbied the legislature to propose an amendment to the state constitution aimed at barring the door to marriage equality. The amendment was ratified in 1998, carving an exception into the state's equal protection clause: "The legislature shall have the power to reserve marriage to opposite sex couples." A year later, the state supreme court ruled that its hands were tied, that despite Judge Chang's finding that the state has no reason for denying licenses, the legal challenge by Ninia and Genora, Joe and Pat, and Toni and Tammy could not continue. The historic Hawaii case came to an end in December 1999, just ten days before the Vermont Supreme Court in turn ruled against discrimination.

Though ultimately Hawaii did not become the first state to end sex discrimination in marriage, the three couples won an important victory, a necessary victory for any civil rights struggle. In the eight years it took the case to wind its way through the Hawaii court system, fair-minded people began, as Abraham Lincoln put it, to "think anew." [37] Before Hawaii, most Americans had never heard the words *gay* and *marriage* in the same sentence. But by September 1999, a *Wall Street Journal* / NBC poll reported that more than two-thirds of Americans had come to believe that gay people will win the freedom to marry. [38]

As we will see in the next chapter, gay Americans are not the first to confront discrimination and exclusion, and not the first to see their civil rights and ability to protect their loved ones contested on the battleground of marriage. What Hawaii did was ask the question, "What is the reason for continuing this discrimination?" As more Americans now ask themselves that same question, the ground plowed by gay couples, such as those in Hawaii, and by non-gay allies who believe in justice for all, such as Dan Foley, is finally beginning to yield its harvest.

CHAPTER THREE

WILL ALLOWING
GAY COUPLES TO MARRY
HARM SOCIETY?

*The strategy to inculturate [sic] active homosexual practice
into our society as a favored institution is synonymous with
injecting a cancer into a healthy body. Homosexual marriage directly attacks the family which is the most vital cell
in society. . . . We must not allow this vital cell, the rock
upon which society is built, to be inculturated with a per-
version that will destroy it, and with it the future of our
children and grandchildren. . . .*
Attorneys for Christian Coalition founder
Pat Robertson (1997)[1]

*I found out the other day that apparently we're allowing
same-sex couples to get married. That is outrageous. Next
thing you know blacks and whites will be using the same
water fountains or Jews will be allowed to own property. . . .
I for one will take to the streets if they even suggest allowing
women to vote. There are limits to freedom and if a woman*

voting isn't one of them, I don't know what is. How dare our Supreme Court decide legal issues? Who do they think they are? Some kind of court that's supreme? We don't need courts trying to hijack our democracy. We can rely on politicians to interpret constitutional legislation. After all, everybody knows politicians never make stupid decisions.

Ike Awgu, *Ottawa Sun* columnist, Canada (2003)[2]

The justices of the Massachusetts Supreme Judicial Court had hardly hung up their robes after issuing their landmark marriage-equality decision in November 2003 when that state's governor, Mitt Romney, declared his biggest quarrel with the majority opinion: The history-making ruling, he said, itself flies in the face of history.

Instead of complying with the constitutional command of equality, Governor Romney said he would lead the charge to amend the Massachusetts state constitution, one of the first constitutions in the world (older than even the United States), written by John Adams himself. The amendment to block marriage equality, the governor told ABC's *Good Morning America,* will "conform [to] three thousand years of human history, saying that marriage is between a man and a woman."[3]

I'm sure many history buffs across the country choked on their morning coffee when they heard this assertion. I was a little surprised, in fact, that *Good Morning America* host Charles Gibson didn't do the same. Three *thousand* years of human history? While I have no doubt that Governor Romney is a well-educated man—he earned degrees from both Harvard and Brigham Young, after all—he seems to have forgotten some important parts of the history of marriage, including its recent history right here in America in our lifetimes.

But since many of the opponents of marriage equality like to make this claim—"marriage has always been between a man and a woman for three, five, six thousand years," depending on the day, "and it shouldn't change"—here are a few years and a few changes in the past millennia of marriage that they are leaving out of the picture, borrowed in part from E. J. Graff's illuminating tour through the history of marriage, *What Is Marriage For? The Strange Social History of Our Most Intimate Institution:*

◆ 950 B.C.: King Solomon follows the tradition of the day, which dictates that lesser kings give a daughter's hand in marriage in order to seal a treaty with a more powerful king, and finds himself with seven hundred wives and three hundred concubines.

◆ 1400 A.D.: Parents in France and Holland have the legal authority to veto a daughter's choice of spouse until she turns twenty-five and a son's choice until he turns thirty.[4]

◆ 1775: Married women lose the right to own property, make contracts, or file lawsuits after Lord Blackstone, widely considered an architect of British common law, declares that "husband and wife are one person, and the husband is that person."[5]

◆ 1863: Alabama passes a law forbidding marriage between members of different races, later enshrined in the state constitution and only removed in the year 2000 (with 40 percent of voters still voting to keep it in).

◆ 1907: Governor Romney's father is born in Chihuahua, Mexico, where Mormon settlers moved, in part to avoid harassment under U.S. laws forbidding polygamy.

Were Romney serious on *Good Morning America,* the history he presumably would be seeking to defend would entitle him to marry the (white) first daughters of the less populated states of Rhode Island, Maine, New Hampshire, and Vermont—submerging their property and legal personhood into his. Such is the history of marriage that the governor claims to "defend."

Or maybe that's not what he had in mind.

Perhaps Romney and other opponents have forgotten all the many changes that have taken place in the institution of marriage throughout history and in recent decades, changes that have taken marriage from being a dynastic or property arrangement to what we think of it as today: a committed union between equals based on love, commitment, self-sacrifice, hope, sharing, companionship, consent, and responsibility for the person of your choice.

Or, more likely, the opponents of marriage equality haven't really forgotten about these changes and battles and are instead, for political purposes, channeling Chicken Little in order to scare Americans away from supporting full marriage equality as the Constitution requires. Just what *will* happen now that Massachusetts, like most of Canada, has ended gay couples' exclusion from marriage? Or when California and Connecticut or New Jersey and Oregon follow suit? Will our neighbors' marriages fail? Will same-sex couples use up all the marriage licenses? Will heterosexuals quit the marriage "club"? Will, as Chicken Little suggested so many times, the sky fall?

As more and more Americans, including more and more judges and journalists, begin asking the question "Just how would it harm someone to allow others to marry?" opponents of gay couples' right to marry have yet to explain exactly what the consequences of ending marriage discrimination against gay people would be, even as they push to plaster discrimination into our federal and state constitutions. Maybe smarter politicians such as Romney don't attempt that extra step of actually explaining because they learned a thing or two from the experience of U.S. Senator Rick Santorum, Republican of Pennsylvania, who took a stab at fleshing out the answer and laid bare the hollowness of the opposition's case.

"If the Supreme Court says that you have the right to consensual sex within your home," Santorum told an Associated Press reporter in April 2003, explaining why he believed the U.S. Supreme Court should not overturn the discriminatory Texas law against private consensual sex for gay Americans,

> then you have the right to bigamy, you have the right to polygamy, you have the right to incest, you have the right to adultery. You have the right to anything. All of those things are antithetical to a healthy, stable, traditional family. And that's sort of where we are in today's world, unfortunately. It all comes from, I would argue, this right to privacy that doesn't exist, in my opinion, in the United States Constitution.

Moving on from his rejection not just of gay people's right to have sex in their own home, but also of the Supreme Court's 1965 right-to-privacy decision in a case involving the right of married heterosexuals to use contraception without government interference, the senator almost offhandedly added, "That's not to pick on homosexuality. It's not, you know, man on child, man on dog, or whatever the case may be." [6]

Senator Santorum's comments were almost immediately understood as extremist by the many Americans—gay and non-gay alike—who believe that the Supreme Court was right to say as long ago as 1965 that choices about whether or not to use contraceptives, or have a family, or have sex, properly belong to individuals, not the government. The AP reporter who was interviewing Santorum at the time admitted to astonishment at the senator's explanation. "I'm sorry, I didn't think I was going to talk about 'man on dog sex' with a United States senator—it's sort of freaking me out," she told Santorum. [7]

Most Americans understand that respecting equality under the law and saying that the government can't dictate the life choices of gay or non-gay couples is what conservatives used to stand for, an affirmation of our American idea of freedom and limited government, not a rush to the "right to anything."

But just how different was the senator's attack on the U.S. Supreme Court from the governor's comments following the Massachusetts marriage ruling? True, Romney didn't repeat Santorum's candid admission that he is not just against gay equality in marriage, but also against choice in contraception and against the right to privacy, too. Ending the denial of marriage rights to gay people won't contradict human history, lead to polygamy or "man on dog" sex, or be a threat to kids, just as it won't lead to the sky falling. And I'd be willing to bet that Governor Romney and Senator Santorum know this just as well as you and I do. They must also know that the only way they are adhering to history in their extraordinary efforts to block the civil rights of gay people is in the "sky is falling" arguments they're employing. These scare tactics are anything but new. Romney and Santorum, like most of the opponents of marriage equality today, are echoing familiar claims from the many past struggles that have taken place (and are still taking place) on the battlefield of marriage rights in America.

Consider, for example, these other examples of gloom and doom compiled in a 1996 column by the *Chicago Tribune*'s Eric Zorn:

1. A Republican senator from Wisconsin says marriages between gay couples must be forbidden "simply because natural instinct revolts at it as wrong."
2. An anti-gay group declares that extending the right to marry to gay couples would result in "a degraded and ignoble population incapable of moral and intellectual development." Group members say they based their stand on the "natural superiority with which God [has] ennobled heterosexuals."

3. A psychologist says "the tendency to classify all persons who oppose gay marriage as 'prejudiced' is in itself prejudice." He added, "Nothing of any significance is gained by such a marriage."

4. A Georgia lawmaker states that allowing gay people to marry "necessarily involves [the] degradation" of conventional marriage, an institution that "deserves admiration rather than execration."

5. A Kentucky congressman warns, "The next step will be that gays and lesbians will demand a law allowing them, without restraint, to . . . have free and unrestrained social intercourse with your unmarried sons and daughters." He adds: "It is bound to come to that. There is no disguising the fact. And the sooner the alarm is given and the people take heed, the better it will be for our civilization."

6. A Missouri judge rules, "When people of the same sex marry, they cannot possibly have any progeny . . . . And such a fact sufficiently justifies those laws which forbid their marriage."

7. A Virginia state law says marriages between gay couples are "abominable" and would "pollute" American society.

8. In denying the appeal of a same-sex couple that tried to marry, a Georgia court rules that such marriages are "not only unnatural, but—always productive of deplorable results," such as increased effeminate behavior in the population. "They are productive of evil, and evil only, without any corresponding good . . . [in accordance with] the God of nature."

9. A congressman from Illinois opines that bans against the freedom to marry are not unconstitutional because they apply "equally to men and women."

10. Attorneys for the state of Tennessee say gay and lesbian couples should be prevented from marrying because they are "distasteful to our people and unfit to produce the human race. . . ." The state supreme court agrees, ruling that extending the freedom to marry would be "a calamity full of the saddest and gloomiest portent to the generations that are to come after us."

11. Lawyers for the state of California say a law preventing gay people from marrying is necessary to prevent "traditional marriage from being contaminated by the recognition of relationships that are physically and mentally inferior [and entered into by] the dregs of society."

12. In response to a lawsuit challenging Virginia's anti-gay-marriage law, a state judge rules, "The law concerning marriages is to be construed and understood in relation to those persons only to whom that law relates . . . and not to a class of person clearly not within the idea of the legislature when contemplating the subject of marriage." [8]

The kicker in Zorn's column is that these twelve statements were not, in fact, made about gay people's freedom to marry. They actually were made between 1823 and 1964 by opponents of interracial marriage and African-Americans' equal citizenship. Zorn replaced the references to race with references to sexual orientation to underscore how today's battle over gay people's freedom to marry is not just about gay and lesbian people. It is a chapter in a civil rights struggle as old as the institution of marriage itself, a struggle that has also been borne by women seeking equality, people seeking to marry others of a different race, adults seeking to make their own decisions about parenting and sex, and married couples seeking an end to failed or abusive unions.

Look again at the twelve statements Eric Zorn quoted and switch them back, replacing the references to sexual orientation with references to race. How absurd it seems today to suggest that interracial couples can't procreate, that they are mentally and physically inferior, or that they cause the contamination of young children's minds. Read as arguments to justify continuing race discrimination in marriage, accepted not so long ago as part of the "definition" of marriage and God's own plan, it is easy to see them today as laughable (until we remember that real people were blocked for centuries in their desire to marry the person of their choice by the laws that opponents of equality fiercely defended).

Now take the exercise a step further. Imagine how preposterous similar statements regarding the need to "defend" marriage against committed gay couples will sound thirty years from now.

If there is one solid lesson about marriage that we can take by examining three thousand years of human history—or by looking across the border to Canada—it is that the sky doesn't fall, even if Niagara Falls still does, when people are able to choose whether and whom to marry, and are accorded equal treatment under the law.

The history of marriage is a history of change. In fact, in our lifetimes, right here in America, there have been at least four major changes in the legal institution of marriage. Each of them was at least as "sweeping," at least as big a departure from the conception and traditions of the day, and at least as hotly contested as is the proposal today to end sex discrimination in marriage.

DIVORCE

As shown by E. J. Graff and others, attitudes for and against divorce have changed almost as many times as the institution of marriage itself. In the sixteenth century, for example, when marriage was an obligation people undertook both for economic purposes and to ensure the continued population of their country and their church, the idea of divorce was practically unspoken. For Catholic couples, it was usually impossible, at least in theory. For Protestant couples, it was an option only if the marriage contract were somehow broken—impeding or violating the sexual element of the marriage. While adultery and refusing to have sex were grounds for divorce, falling out of love never was.[9]

Some of these standards, particularly the Protestant ones, were the basis of U.S. divorce law, too, making it virtually unheard of for couples to separate legally once they had tied the knot. And even when divorces were granted, they were seldom easy to achieve. While some states gave the courts authority over the process, others, particularly in the South, required case-by-case approval by a vote of the legislature. (Can you imagine!)

As society in the mid-nineteenth century began to embrace our nation's commitment to individual freedom—and the idea that men and women deserve to be happy in their marriages and actually love their spouse—the laws preventing divorce began to crumble . . . though not without controversy, at least on the right.

When Connecticut changed its divorce law in 1816, Yale University President Timothy Dwight packed a lot into a stern warning:

> Within a moderate period, the whole community will be thrown, by laws made in open opposition to the Laws of God, into general prostitution. . . . To the Eye of God, those who are polluted in each of these modes [divorce and prostitution], are alike, and equally impure, loathsome, abandoned wretches; and are the offspring of Sodom and Gomorrah.[10]

Another such controversy erupted after 1850, when Indiana passed the most liberal divorce law the country had yet seen. Judges could grant divorces for any reason, and a man from out of state only needed to check into an Indiana hotel and stay there for an hour before he was eligible for residency, which was required for him to be granted a divorce.[11] As you might imagine, Indiana became the first divorce capital of the United States. In 1858, the *Indiana Daily Journal* complained, "We are overrun by a flock of ill-used and ill-using, petulant, libidinous, extravagant, ill-fitting husbands and wives as a sink is overrun with the foul water of the whole house."[12]

Indiana eventually dammed the flow of "foul water" by tightening its residency requirements. But other states picked up the slack—most notably Nevada, for those of you who remember George Cukor's 1939 camp classic, *The Women,* a movie that was centered partly on a Reno "divorce ranch." Still, most states required that a couple show acceptable grounds for seeking a divorce and that both the husband and the wife agree to the divorce before their marriage was granted a legal end. The law continued to evolve, reflecting the understanding that as painful as breakups might be, marriage really should be based on consent and commitment, not compulsion.

Ironically, in today's America, it is the states in the South and the "Bible Belt" that have the highest rates of divorce—not Massachusetts, California, Vermont, or New Jersey. Yet right-wing opponents, many of whom claim to be speaking in the name of religion, lash out again and again at gay people and states leading the way toward equal respect for all families, while turning a blind eye to the failures or problems within their own ranks.

More than any other change, allowing a freedom to divorce and respecting people's choice were major departures from the "tradition," the conception, the history of marriage, and from some people's view of "God's law." More than any other change, divorce clearly does have an impact on families and kids, as necessary and proper as divorce often is. But it's because most Americans have come to understand that divorce can indeed often be the right, if regrettable, choice, and because most Americans understand that the decision to divorce should be made by the couple involved rather than by politicians, that we don't see Senator Santorum, Governor Romney, or the White House pushing a constitutional amendment on divorce.

WOMEN AS LEGALLY SUBORDINATE TO THEIR HUSBANDS

For much of this country's early history, government enforced the common law rule of "coverture" when it came to marriages. This doctrine, by which a woman's identity was "covered" by that of her husband—essentially reducing her to his chattel or property—grew out of civilization's agrarian period, when a family was dependent on all of its members to make the family business, the farm, work effectively and efficiently. To maintain social order at a time when only men could vote, society gave husbands the preeminent authority at home as well.

The husband's absolute authority required that his wife give up all of hers upon exchanging vows. Any property she owned, whether she acquired it before or after the marriage, became his. And because the husband was the sole representative of his family unit, married women also lost their rights as citizens to sign contracts or to sue or be sued individually.

Just as the Industrial Revolution dismantled society's agrarian patterns, it encouraged women to stand up to these archaic legal doctrines. As women took their place in city sweatshops, they balked when their husbands pocketed their paltry wages. It was especially galling when even cheating—or imprisoned—men could stake legal claim on their wives' take-home pay, as was the case in

1857, when a Massachusetts court ruled that a man who was in jail was still entitled to his wife's labor, and money.[13]

As women increasingly started earning their own keep, state legislatures began chipping away at the coverture doctrine by passing a series of Married Women's Property Laws, which in turn provoked a slew of gloom and doom predictions of how property-owning wives would mean the demise of marriage and the family unit. E. J. Graff describes how in 1844 a New York legislative committee stated that women's independence would lead to "infidelity in the marriage bed, a high rate of divorce, and increased female criminality," redefining marriage from "its high and holy purposes" into something solely about "convenience and sensuality."[14] Meanwhile, a Maryland judge refused to recognize his state's Married Women's Property Law, stating that the law would destroy the "moral and social efficacy of the marriage institution. . . . What incentive would there be for such a wife ever to reconcile differences with her husband, to act in submission to his wishes, and perform the many onerous duties pertaining to her sphere? Would not every wife . . . abandon her husband and her home?"[15] What incentive, indeed?

Vestiges of this legal subordination of women in marriage lasted a long, long time—think about how the tradition of "Mr. and Mrs. Him" comes from the idea that a man's identity "covers" his wife. As late as 1976 a Massachusetts court was asked to decide if a wife, under common law, could sue her husband. (The court decided that yes, she could, but note it was a matter of doubt as recently as the Bicentennial.)[16] I myself, as a young attorney, worked on the case that ended what was called the "marital rape exemption" in New York—the rule, at one time pervasive throughout the states, that a man could not be prosecuted for raping his wife and taking what "belonged to him" as a husband. That was not some ancient past; that was 1984 in "liberal" New York.

Despite the broader agenda of the opponents of marriage equality for gays—an agenda very much alive, as shown by the 1998 Southern Baptist Convention's call for the woman "to submit herself graciously to the servant leadership of her husband"—most Americans today would not urge (at least not in front of their wives or daughters) that our country return to this tradition of marriage, no matter how "efficient" it made the family unit or how much it conformed to some religious views of "God's plan" and the "definition of marriage."

MARRIAGE AND CHOICES
ABOUT SEX AND PARENTING

It was again the shift from an agrarian economy to an industrial base, as well as medical and technological innovations and expanding notions of liberty, that prompted changes in the relationship between procreation and marriage. If the "bigger the brood the better the harvest" credo was no longer necessary, why should a woman be tied to bearing the burden of that brood? Couldn't women have more freedom to shape their lives, whether while raising children or without them? Shouldn't women and men enjoy companionship and sexual fulfillment in their marriage without risking unwanted pregnancy?

Following many fierce battles over the morality of contraception and claims that it would destroy marriage and civilization, people began going to court to get the government out of their marital bedroom. Again, there was gloom and doom from the opponents on the right. As historian David Garrow relates in his excellent book *Liberty and Sexuality: The Right to Privacy and the Making of Roe v. Wade,* one commentator declared that "Japanese birth control devices in the homes of America can be more destructive than Japanese bombers over Pearl Harbor," while bishops and their allies testifying before the Connecticut Legislature warned that if restrictions on contraception were removed, "within twenty-five years the state will be a mass of smoldering ruins." [17]

In its 1965 decision in *Griswold v. Connecticut,* the U.S. Supreme Court made clear that in America, at least, marriage is based on choice and respect for the couple, not the government's agenda or religious doctrines about procreation. "Would we allow the police to search the sacred precincts of marital bedrooms for telltale signs of the use of contraceptives?" Justice William O. Douglas wrote for the Court.

> We deal with a right of privacy older than the Bill of Rights—older than our political parties, older than our school system. Marriage is a coming together for better or for worse, hopefully enduring, and intimate to the degree of being sacred. It is an association that promotes a way of life, not causes; a harmony in living, not political faiths; a bilateral loyalty, not commercial or social projects. Yet it is an association for as noble a purpose as any involved in our prior decisions. [18]

Who could argue with that? How current is this battle over marriage and choice? As we discussed earlier in this chapter, it was as recently as April 2003 that Senator Santorum interrupted his anti-gay tirade to attack *Griswold,* the constitutional right to privacy, and non-gay as well as gay Americans' freedom to make their own decisions about, yes, contraception.

RACE DISCRIMINATION IN MARRIAGE

Six of the original thirteen colonies had laws banning marriages between people of different races, specifically between white people and African-Americans. But as Nancy Cott explains in her book

Public Vow: A History of Marriage and the Nation, race discrimination in marriage had exploded across the country by the start of the Civil War. In 1860, when there were only thirty-three states, twenty-three states and U.S. territories banned interracial marriages. Many of those states without specific laws were in the South, where stricter slave codes made explicit racial bans "unnecessary" until after the war, at which time marriage discrimination was codified there, too.[19]

In many of these states, African-Americans were not permitted to marry at all; as a further mark of dehumanization, their commitments to one another were deemed unworthy of the respect and status of marriage. Resilient couples developed their own ceremonies of commitment (such as "jumping the broom," a ritual slaves derived from African traditions) and, of course, manifested love, devotion, and fidelity. But their personal commitment had no legal weight, and by "definition" and law, they could not marry. Similar restrictions forbidding Chinese people and others from marrying existed in a handful of states at various points in American history.

These laws, which gave government the authority to determine who was—or was not—an appropriate spouse, represented popularly held beliefs about the institution of marriage at the time, as Eric Zorn showed in his *Chicago Tribune* column. And, as Zorn also pointed out, there was strong political and social opposition to changing these laws to better reflect the country's increasing awareness of individual freedom generally, as well as in marriage. Courts routinely rubber-stamped discrimination in marriage with recourse to sweeping assertions about the "definition" of marriage, claims of what is natural or "unnatural," attacks on the people seeking to marry the "wrong" kind of partner, and predictions that marriage equality would lead to disaster. As one typical ruling put it:

The amalgamation of the races is not only unnatural, but is always productive of deplorable results. Our daily observations show us that the offspring of these unnatural connections are generally sickly and effeminate. . . . Such connections never elevate the inferior race to the position of the superior, but they bring down the superior to that of the inferior. They are productive of evil, and evil only, without any corresponding good.[20]

This is what the majority of people believed for a long, long time, and until fairly recently—as deeply and sincerely as some oppose marriage equality for same-sex couples today. This is the way in which the law of marriage was used to enforce and perpetuate not just inequality, but the prejudice itself.

It took until 1948 before any court in the country mustered the commitment to the constitutional mandate of equality for all and the courage to reject political and social pressure in order to strike down race discrimination in marriage. With its 4–3 decision in *Perez v. Sharp,* the California Supreme Court entered history as an example of a court willing to stand up for justice in the case before it, without fear or favor, unswayed by those who urged it to "connive at infractions" of constitutional guarantees and the human dignity of a vulnerable minority.[21] And in doing so, it set an example for the courts doing their job in Hawaii, Vermont, and Massachusetts half a century later and immeasurably enriched our nation.

Each person seeking a license to marry the "wrong" kind of person, the justices said, "finds himself barred by law from marrying the person of his choice and that person to him may be irreplaceable. Human beings are bereft of worth and dignity by a doctrine that would make them as interchangeable as trains."[22] The courageous California Supreme Court decision in *Perez* marked the beginning of the end of race discrimination in marriage, much as the November 2003 decision of the Massachusetts high court, similarly 4–3, marked the beginning of the end of sex discrimination in marriage.

The *Perez* decision came a full nineteen years before the U.S. Supreme Court overturned antimiscegenation laws nationwide in the best-named case ever, *Loving v. Virginia.* The *Perez* decision came before a right-wing campaign to amend the California Constitution to block civil rights laws and tie the hands of so-called "activist judges," and before the U.S. Supreme Court decision rejecting such efforts to subvert equality. It also came before legislators in most states (including California) were willing to stand against discrimination and before the polls showed the public's acceptance of equality in marriage or other civil rights. But some state had to show leadership. The California Supreme Court did not flinch; in the best tradition of American courts, it did its job, and history has upheld it.

When the question of race discrimination in marriage came again before the U.S. Supreme Court (the Court had actually gotten it wrong in previous decades and ducked the question repeatedly in the years following *Perez*),[23] it was in a 1967 case brought by a black woman, Mildred Jeter, and a white man, Richard Loving. The couple had had to leave their home state, Virginia, in order to get married where their love was allowed. The law in Virginia, like that of many other states, provided: "All marriages between a white person and a colored person shall be absolutely void without any decree of divorce or other legal process." An interracial marriage was considered a nonstarter, contrary to the very "definition" of marriage.

Back from their honeymoon, the Lovings were arrested one night in their own bedroom—with their wedding certificate hanging over their bed—and prosecuted for the "crime" of "evading" their state's discriminatory law and violating Virginia's same-race restriction on marriage. Mildred and Richard were convicted of marrying the "wrong" kind of person. Their marriage was pronounced an un-marriage, and they were given a choice of a year in prison or twenty-five years' exile from their home state. They chose exile, got a lawyer, and sued to defend their family. The Lovings lost in state courts all the way up; the trial judge went so far as to declare: "Almighty God created the races white, black, yellow, Malay, and red, and he placed them on separate continents[.] The fact that he separated the races shows that he did not intend for the races to mix." The Virginia Supreme Court upheld the discriminatory "definition" of marriage, and the case came before the U.S. Supreme Court, which reversed, declaring, "The freedom to marry has long been recognized as one of the vital personal rights essential to the orderly pursuit of happiness by free men."[24]

Today this seems self-evident, but remember that when the California Supreme Court struck down discrimination in marriage, polls showed 90 percent of the public opposed marriage equality for interracial couples. As late as 1967, when the U.S. Supreme Court finally got *Loving* right, the polls showed 70 percent opposed.[25] Imagine the injury to our nation if the opposition had prevailed with arguments like "let the people vote" or with attacks on "activist judges," and had cemented discrimination into our Constitution. Would we ever have secured the equality and freedom that most of us consider to be our nation's commitment and defining greatness?

* * *

Decades after these revolutions in marriage, the controversies surrounding the changes are hard for many of us to believe, and yet (ask Senator Santorum) these same controversies are still very alive. Most if not all of us agree that the changes were important and right. And few if any of us would want to go back to a time when marriage was the way it was before—before couples could divorce, before women could speak for themselves, before marriage was understood as a relationship of consent and equality, before married couples decided for themselves when and whether they would have children, and before the repeal of laws saying you could not marry someone of the "wrong" race because of the "definition" of marriage.

And viewed from the distance of time, we can see that society was not hurt by these changes, despite the discomfort, scare tactics, and threats at the time. Quite to the contrary, society is, in fact, stronger because of these changes. Alarms such as those sounded today by Governor Mitt Romney, Senator Rick Santorum, and other opponents of marriage equality have been made and exposed as false time and time again, after much needless divisiveness and harm to families in our country.

In fact, as conservative columnist Ramesh Ponnuru pointed out in a recent column in the *National Journal,* claims that ending marriage discrimination against same-sex couples will lead to a parade of horribles are a sign of political weakness. "Doom and gloom" arguments are an acknowledgment that equal marriage rights for gay couples are "not self-evidently objectionable, but [have] to be condemned because [they] would lead to other, more objectionable things." [26] Slippery-slope diversions are what opponents of equality try when they don't have a good reason to justify ongoing discrimination, the equivalent of a lawyer with no arguments and no evidence pounding the table.

We needn't wait for time to refute Romney's mischaracterization of three thousand years of human history. And we don't have to wait decades to show that "more objectionable things" won't follow the decision to grant marriage equality to gay couples. We can look at our own history and be grateful that our country ended marriage discrimination in the past. We can look to the Netherlands, Belgium, or Canada, where same-sex couples already have the freedom to marry and families have been helped while no one is hurt. And, indeed, we can look in our own neighborhoods—where gay families are increasingly welcomed and more clearly understood as contributing to society—and see that the sky is not falling.

CHAPTER FOUR

ISN'T MARRIAGE FOR PROCREATION?

Marriage is not about affirming somebody's love for somebody else. It's about uniting together to be open to children, to further civilization in our society.

U.S. Senator Rick Santorum (R-Pennsylvania) [1]

Our laws of civil marriage do not privilege procreative heterosexual intercourse between married people above every other form of adult intimacy and every other means of creating a family. . . . Even people who cannot stir from their deathbed may marry. While it is certainly true that many, perhaps most, married couples have children together (assisted or unassisted), it is the exclusive and permanent commitment of the marriage partners to one another, not the begetting of children, that is the sine qua non of civil marriage.

Massachusetts Supreme Judicial Court,
Goodridge v. Department of Public Health (2003) [2]

If you go to any of the hundreds of fundamentalist Web sites on the Internet today, you have a good chance of coming across a list of talking points against "same-sex marriage." One such script, put together by the Christian radio show *Point of View,* gives thirteen reasons why listeners should be opposed to gay couples' freedom to marry. High on the list is a lesson in "basic biology." According to *Point of View*'s script, anti-marriage-equality activists are supposed to say, "Homosexual relations deny the self-evident truth that male and female bodies complement each other. Human sexuality and procreation is based upon a man and a woman coming together as one flesh. Marriage between a man and a woman promotes procreation and makes intimate sexual activity orderly and socially accountable."[3]

Let's put aside for the time being the objections many of us, gay and non-gay alike, probably have to the totalitarian notion that intimate sexual activity should be "orderly and socially accountable." Focus, instead, on the rest of the scripted answer, which, if it were rephrased, might read like one of those analytical word problems on a college entrance exam: "If it's a given that the primary purpose of marriage is having children, and it's a given that only a man and a woman—together—can biologically have a child, shouldn't marriage be solely about the union of two different-sex people?"

At first glance, the "basic biology" argument seems to make some sense. After all, it doesn't take more than a fourth-grade health class education to know that men's and women's bodies in some sense "complement each other" and that when a man and a woman come "together as one flesh" it often leads to procreation.

In fact, the "basic biology" argument makes enough sense at first glance that it was used in each of this country's high-profile cases against the freedom to marry—first in Hawaii and then in Vermont and Massachusetts. In each case, attorneys for the state said the government's interest in basic biology, or in "promoting procreation," was a primary reason—if not the only justification—for prohibiting gay couples from getting married.

In 1994, Hawaii argued that the state's marriage law could be traced all the way back to an 1846 decree by King Kamehameha III, who, the state contended, meant for marriage to promote procreation between a man and a woman. (The state failed even to acknowledge Hawaii's older, pre-Christian tradition of *aikane,* which involved taking a same-sex partner instead of—or sometimes along with—a wife. Kamehameha the Great, who first unified the islands, himself had an *aikane* partner, a high chief named Kuakini.)[4] "There is a mystical bond between a mother, a father, and their child," the state instead told the court. "The purpose of the marriage law is to encourage procreation through male-female marriages. . . . No same-sex couples, as a couple, can have children."[5]

In 1998, lawyers for Vermont agreed with the plaintiffs that gay people have a fundamental right to marry, but they said the right extends only so far as to allow them to marry someone of the other sex, regardless of love.[6] "To say [otherwise] would be to say there's absolutely no connection between marriage and procreation," the state's attorneys told the state supreme court. "It's a unique social institution based on the sexual communion of a man and a woman."[7]

And in 2003, lawyers for the commonwealth of Massachusetts said the state can forbid gay couples from marrying because "limiting marriage to opposite-sex couples furthers the state's interest in fostering the link between marriage and procreation."[8]

Because the "basic biology" argument just seems so, well, basic, I understand why some people want to stop right there. But, as I'm sure many of you have already realized, the overstated link between procreation and marriage actually doesn't explain why we bar same-sex couples (and same-sex couples alone) from marriage as it now exists under law and in our society. In fact, once you scratch the surface of this argument—which is actually more of a gut feeling than a thought-out rationale—you can see that it's riddled with holes. And thankfully, these are holes that the justices in Hawaii, Vermont, and Massachusetts saw right through.

In Hawaii, Judge Kevin Chang returned to the analysis of marriage put forward by Justice Sandra Day O'Connor, writing for the unanimous U.S. Supreme Court in its 1987 ruling in *Turner v. Safley*. As we discussed in chapter 1, the Supreme Court noted that prisoners, whose incarceration might keep them from having sex with a spouse (and thus, in turn, prevent them from having biological children), might have many other reasons for wanting to exercise their constitutional freedom to marry. Significantly, the Supreme Court did not include conceiving or raising children on its list of the "important attributes" of marriage under the law.

Twelve years later in the Hawaii freedom-to-marry case that Dan Foley and I litigated, Judge Chang wrote:

In Hawaii, and elsewhere, people marry for a variety of reasons including, but not limited to the following: (1) having or raising children; (2) stability and commitment; (3) emotional closeness; (4) intimacy and monogamy; (5) the establishment of a framework for a long-term relationship; (6) personal significance; (7) recognition by society; and (8) certain legal and economic protections, benefits and obligations.[9]

"Gay men and lesbian women," the judge found, "share this same *mix* of reasons for wanting to be able to marry," a mix that may include having, or caring for, one's kids, but often does not, and that for many couples turns on other important aspects of marriage.

In Vermont, Chief Justice Jeffrey Amestoy seemed to find it hard to take the state's "procreation" argument seriously. If Vermont truly based a couple's competency to marry on that couple's ability to procreate, he suggested, state officials might want to take a second look at some of the marriage licenses they have been issuing.

> It is . . . undisputed that many opposite-sex couples marry for reasons unrelated to procreation, that some of these couples never intend to have children, and that others are incapable of having children. Therefore, if the purpose of the statutory exclusion of same-sex couples is to "further the link between procreation and child rearing," it is significantly under-inclusive. The law extends the benefits and protections of marriage to many persons with no logical connection to the stated governmental goal.[10]

And in Massachusetts, Chief Justice Margaret Marshall didn't even wait to write the court's decision in the case before letting the state's attorneys know what she thought about their use of the "promotion of procreation" as Massachusetts' justification for excluding gay couples from marriage.

"I think it would be a stretch to say it was for procreation," she said to the state's lawyers during the oral argument. "The State is free to say, for example, after a heterosexual couple has been married for ten years and has produced no children, unless there is evidence that both are infertile, that they should be divorced so that they can be free to marry to try and procreate with another couple?" Despite the asserted link between marriage and procreation put forward to justify excluding gay couples, the state refused to apply any such link to heterosexuals: "For the State to draw the line that way would be an impermissible intrusion into the private lives of the people involved," the assistant attorney general replied (giving no similar weight to the intrusiveness of denying gay people the right to marry and make their own parenting and personal choices like non-gay couples).

Chief Justice Marshall then pointed out that Massachusetts (like Vermont) not only allows nonprocreative couples to marry and stay married, but also permits gay parents to adopt, has many parents who conceived their children through alternative insemination and other means, and has a strong public policy of supporting kids, no matter who their parents are or what their family configuration is.[11]

Indeed, even U.S. Supreme Court Justice Antonin Scalia, hardly a proponent of equal rights for gay men and lesbians, wrote in his 2003 dissent to *Lawrence v. Texas* that the promotion of procreation is a very weak argument for maintaining bans on gay people's freedom to marry. "If moral disapprobation of homosexual conduct is 'no state interest' for purposes of proscribing [private adult sex]," Scalia wrote, "what justification could there possibly be for denying the benefits of marriage to homosexual couples? Surely not the encouragement of procreation, since the sterile and the elderly are allowed to marry."[12]

Actually, the Supreme Court's drawing of a distinction between marriage and procreation goes beyond *Lawrence v. Texas* in 2003 and *Turner v. Safley* in 1987. To hear the opponents of gay equality today, one would not know that for decades the law of the land (America, that is, unlike more theocratic or women-subordinating societies) has been to recognize that marriage is not just about procreation—indeed, is not necessarily about procreation at all.

The Court recognized the right *not* to procreate in marriage, a personal choice protected in a free society under the Constitution, as early as *Eisenstadt v. Baird* in 1972 and *Griswold v. Connecticut* in 1965. In such cases, the justices ruled that government officials could not block a couple—married or unmarried—from making their own decisions about procreation, sex, and the use of contraception. "If the right to privacy means anything," the court ruled in *Eisenstadt*, "it is the right of the individual, married or single, to be free from unwarranted governmental intrusion into matters so fundamentally affecting a person as the decision whether to bear or beget a child." [13]

Given these legal precedents, are Senator Santorum and other opponents correct in saying that "[m]arriage is not about affirming somebody's love for somebody else"?[14] Or is that some other century's, some other country's idea of what the freedom to marry means?

But now let's put these constitutional, legal, and historical understandings of marriage and love aside for a moment and instead focus on some of the commonsense reasons why the procreation argument doesn't work to explain or justify the denial of gay people's freedom to marry. First there is the point raised by Vermont's Chief Justice Amestoy and by U.S. Supreme Court Justice Scalia: No state requires that non-gay couples prove that they can procreate—or promise that they will procreate—before issuing them a marriage license. Indeed, no state requires as a condition of a valid marriage that a couple promises to even engage in sexual intercourse, which would be required for traditional procreation.

And when states issue marriage licenses, none of them come with a "sunset provision," whereby a couple has two or three years to produce a child or the marriage expires. Just imagine how such a law could put millions of marriages in jeopardy. Bob and Elizabeth

Dole, John and Teresa Heinz Kerry, and Pat and Shelley Buchanan are just a few of the married couples that would be forced to divorce by such a law. And certainly George Washington, the Father of Our Country, who never had any children with his wife, Martha, would have objected to such a procreation requirement—a requirement our opponents seem only to conjure up when they seek to deny marriage licenses to gay couples.

Every U.S. state routinely issues marriage licenses to elderly, sterile, and even impotent couples. No state requires them to procreate or to raise children; states recognize that these couples have many other reasons for wanting to marry, including, yes, love, adult companionship, mutual caring and support, and personal commitment.

Meanwhile, every state also recognizes that these and other couples can, and very often do, become parents through adoption or any of a number of other approaches to child-bearing, including donor insemination and surrogacy. The "basic biology" argument ignores that gay and lesbian couples do have, and will continue to have, children by these same means.

And many gay and lesbian parents are raising children they may have conceived during other relationships. Remember Antoinette Pregil, one of the Hawaii marriage plaintiffs? Together with her partner, Tammy Rodrigues, Toni raised her biological daughter, Leina'ala. Leina'ala was only four years old when her mothers met. Fourteen years later she graduated from high school with honors. "I honestly don't think there's a difference" between two different-sex parents or two same-sex parents, Tammy told the Associated Press after the state of Hawaii asserted that gay couples cannot procreate and are not the "optimal" parents. "You can have a mother and a father or you can have a child being brought up with all the love. To me, it's the love."[15]

And how about Hillary and Julie Goodridge? Plaintiffs in the

Massachusetts freedom-to-marry case, they were a committed couple for several years when, in anticipation of the birth of their daughter, Annie, they took the shared last name Goodridge to help bond their growing family and acknowledge their increased and shared family responsibilities. "We want to get married because we love each other and we want to make our family as strong as it could be," Julie told *People* magazine.[16]

And then there are Richard Linnell and Gary Chalmers, who joined Hillary and Julie as plaintiffs in Massachusetts. The men had been together fourteen years and are fathers to a teenage daughter, Paige, whom they adopted as an infant. "I shouldn't have to explain to [Paige] that her parents aren't married, but love each other very much and the three of us are a family," Gary said in a statement released by Gay & Lesbian Advocates & Defenders, the plaintiffs' stellar lawyers. "This shouldn't be a complicated conversation. We have the same concerns, the same routines as any other parents, and we should be recognized and treated in the same way."[17]

In short, while marriage may not be right or available for every parent, most people do choose to have children within the context of marriage. Raising their kids within marriage is precisely what many gay people are seeking to do, despite attacks on their families from the very groups that constantly claim to be "pro-family." Of the thirteen plaintiff couples in the freedom-to-marry cases in Hawaii, Vermont, and Massachusetts, six of them are parents, with seven children between them. Preventing these and other gay and lesbian couples from accessing the tangible and intangible protections and responsibilities of marriage does nothing to help these parents or their kids, nor does it facilitate or encourage procreation by any other group of people. Presumably, non-gay men and women will continue to procreate and marry, even once gay men and lesbians are treated equally. That's why court after court has determined what common sense and a moment's honest reflection reveal: that "basic biology" is no reason to block gay and lesbian couples from marriage.

In fact, if we as a society care about kids—real kids, not just rhetorical children used as a weapon in a culture war—then we have to acknowledge that same-sex couples do have children and those children, it follows, have gay parents. In fact, at least eight thousand children in Massachusetts are being raised by parents in same-sex couples, reported one 2004 study,[18] and researchers analyzing census data have concluded that as many as one in five gay male couples, and one in three lesbian couples, are raising kids.[19]

Basic biology or not, those kids, too, deserve protection and security. It simply makes no sense to, on the one hand, say, "We care about children," and then, on the other hand, punish some kids for having the "wrong parents" by denying their families marriage and its many benefits.[20]

Let's explore this point—the real best interests of real kids, who are, after all, more important than mere rhetoric about biology—further in the next chapter.

CHAPTER FIVE

WHAT ABOUT
THE CHILDREN?

To the extent that the State's purpose in licensing civil marriage was, and is, to legitimize children and provide for their security, the statutes plainly exclude many same-sex couples who are no different from opposite-sex couples with respect to these objectives. If anything, the exclusion of same-sex couples from the legal protections incident to marriage exposes their children to the precise risks that the State argues the marriage laws are designed to secure against.

Vermont Supreme Court, *Baker v. Vermont* (1999)[1]

Nobody can say that their family is a real family and my family is just a bunch of people living in the same house.

Robbie Barnett-Kemper, eleven, the day
his moms married in Canada (2003)

According to the U.S. Census Bureau, there were at least 600,000 gay and lesbian couples living together in the United States in 2000, in virtually every county in the country. At least 180,000 of those couples were raising children.[2] Nearly everyone agrees that the Census Bureau drastically underestimated the actual number of gay families in the country (especially if you consider the number of couples who aren't open about their sexual orientation or their relationship).[3] But if you were to ask some politicians and pundits, even the lowest number of gay couples with children is too many. Disapproving of same-sex relationships, they proceed to assert that children fare best when raised by a mother and a father.

Florida Governor Jeb Bush said as much in January 2004. After a federal court upheld that state's law prohibiting gay people from adopting children—the only such flat-out ban left in the country—the governor issued a statement indicating that he was pleased with the ruling, which was appealed by gay parents and the ACLU. "It is in the best interest of adoptive children, many of whom come from troubled and unstable backgrounds, to be placed in a home anchored by a mother and a father," Governor Bush said, ignoring the fact that gay Floridians are allowed to serve as foster parents while the ban on adoption denies many of these kids the chance to have any permanent parents at all.[4]

Like Bush, Massachusetts state Representative Eugene L. O'Flaherty said it was his overwhelming interest in children's welfare that prompted him to propose legislation, not to improve schools, increase funding for Head Start programs, or assure health coverage for uninsured kids, but rather to reinforce the exclusion of gay couples from marriage. His justifications, he told the *Boston Herald,* include "procreation, family stability, the preservation of the family as a social unit, and studies showing that children do better when raised by a mother and father."[5]

Syndicated columnist and anti-marriage-equality activist Maggie Gallagher is such a proponent of mother- and father-led families that she has said legalized polygamy is preferable to granting gay and lesbian couples the right to marry. "At least polygamy, for all its ugly defects, is an attempt to secure stable mother-father families for children," Gallagher declared as she campaigned for a constitutional amendment to deepen marriage discrimination against same-sex couples.[6]

Meanwhile, Brian S. Brown, the executive director of the Family Institute of Connecticut, told readers of the *Hartford Courant* that "many, many studies support the idea that children do best with both a mother and a father." Brown's proof? "As David Popenoe, social sciences dean at Rutgers University, has emphatically stated, 'I know of few other bodies of data in which the weight of evidence is so decisively on one side of the issue: On the whole, for children, two-parent [mother and father] families are preferable,' " wrote Brown.[7]

Let's take another look at these contentions, especially this one by the Family Institute. (So many of the right wing's anti-gay, anti-choice organizations like to use the word *family* while devoting the lion's share of their time and money not, say, to promoting health insurance or support for children, but rather to attacking gay families and legal rights, as documented in a series of reports by the National Gay and Lesbian Task Force.)[8]

For instance, sociologist David Popenoe, a researcher often cited by right-wing figures, actually said, "On the whole, for children, two-parent families are preferable." It was the Family Institute's Brown who then added the words "mother and father" to the quotation. (Notice the brackets above?) In other words, the Family Institute blatantly twisted the statement to make a scholar's conclusion fit its own particular agenda, the claim that gay and lesbian couples don't make the best of parents and, therefore, should not be granted equal marriage rights.

And, whether or not they're using brackets, Governor Bush, Representative O'Flaherty, Maggie Gallagher, and the anti-gay campaigners are twisting the facts just as much. That's because leading experts and major studies do *not* say children fare better with a mother and a father.

What these experts and studies do say, as Popenoe did, is that children, *on average,* do better when raised by *two parents*—not because single parents are bad or uncaring, but because, all things being equal, two parents means more resources, more support, more help. And those parents, experts including the American Academy of Pediatrics agree, can be a mother and father, or two mothers, or two fathers.

I witnessed a similar effort to twist the facts back in 1996 when Dan Foley and I were in court for the Hawaii marriage trial. Remember, the main argument the state's attorneys had come up with for excluding gay couples from marriage was the claim that the "best" family configuration is a married man and woman with kids. (Attorneys for Vermont and Massachusetts attempted the same argument in the marriage cases in those states.) But a huge problem with this argument, and one of the big reasons it didn't hold up in court, was that it misrepresented the evidence. The state's own witnesses were forced to concede under cross-examination that, while two parents are usually (though not always) better than one, the two can certainly be of the same sex. The experts on both sides agreed that the strength of a family and the quality of parenting are best defined by love, commitment, responsibility, and self-sacrifice, not by the sex of the parents.

Speaking to a reporter in 2004 and reflecting back on his 1996 trial testimony, one of the state's leading witnesses, child psychiatrist Kyle Pruett,

> remember[ed] telling Hawaii's deputy attorney general, "I could just as easily be testifying for the other side." Pruett, director of medical studies at Yale University's Child Study Center, said that theoretically, "it is best to have a mother and a father who are biologically connected and who the state supports in raising the child. But once you move from the theoretical to the practical[,] it is the quality of the relationship that children have with their parents that is far more determinative of their eventual life outcome." [9]

Scholarly researchers such as Andrew Cherlin of Johns Hopkins University, Frank Furstenberg of the University of Pennsylvania, Sara McLanahan of Princeton University, Gary Sandefur and Lawrence Wu of the University of Wisconsin, had conducted most of the studies that Hawaii's attorneys relied on to defend the marriage exclusion. But when these leading experts saw how their work was being mischaracterized, they came together to file a brief on behalf of the plaintiff couples pointing it out.

The scholars wrote:

> Based largely on the premise that research shows that two biological parents or opposite-sex parents comprise a so-called "optimal" child-rearing environment, the State argued at trial that the well-being of children would be harmed if same-sex couples were allowed to marry. [We] would like to advise the

court that it was improper for the State to infer such a conclusion. Because none of the data sources from which this research derives permit identification of same-sex couples or of children residing in same-sex couple families, this research provides no scientifically valid basis for concluding—or even suggesting—that outcomes for children raised by same-sex parents differ from those raised by opposite-sex parents.[10]

Quite to the contrary, the experts wrote, the children of some same-sex couples may even have some advantage because of the hoops their parents had to jump through to conceive them, adopt them, or bring them into the family by other means. "In contrast with the substantial fraction of the nation's children who are unintended and/or unwanted, children born to or adopted by same-sex couples are clearly intended and wanted," they reported.

The actions such couples must take in order to become parents typically include artificial insemination or adoption, either of which requires extensive effort and personal commitment. The fact that same-sex couples who choose to marry and have children are "self-selected" on these and other behavioral characteristics suggests that such couples will, on average, differ from opposite-sex parents in having greater commitment both to one another and to raising children, and that benefits will accrue to their children accordingly.[11]

In 1999, Michael Wald, a Stanford University law professor and former director of the San Francisco Department of Social Services, took an extensive look at the various research studies of the children of gay and lesbian couples. He reported that all the diverse studies worldwide were remarkably consistent in their findings. First, Wald found, the researchers looked at the aspects of childhood development that are of the most concern to the community as a whole. Are the children of gay and lesbian parents more likely to use drugs? Do they have more early pregnancies, suffer more emotional problems, and do they run away from home more often? Do they have more trouble adjusting to adulthood or finding steady employment once they become adults?[12]

Next, the studies looked at the more personal aspects of a child's development. Are the children of gay and lesbian parents happy? How strong is their self-esteem? Do they get along with their parents?[13]

Wald summarized the evidence: None of the studies found that the children of lesbian or gay parents experienced "emotional, intellectual, or social development problems because of their parents' sexual orientation." None of the children of gay parents in the studies had more trouble getting along with their families, had any more difficulty in school, suffered any additional self-esteem problems, or were in any way more likely to engage in self-destructive behavior than the children raised by heterosexual parents. In addition, a study that followed the children of gay and lesbian parents from birth through adulthood found that these kids' ability to transition into adulthood and to find employment in no way differed from children raised by heterosexual parents.[14]

"These children's lives were not problem-free," Wald wrote. But, in essence, the kids "had learned to deal with the fact that society considered their family different, just as children living in other minority families, for example religious minorities or interracial families, learn to cope with community stigma based on their family's difference."[15]

Likewise, the American Psychological Association reported in 1995, upon reviewing the body of studies, that children raised by gay parents are not "disadvantaged in any significant respect relative to the children of heterosexual parents."[16] Since then, most of the nation's leading organizations devoted to children's health, children's welfare, and mental health have declared that a parent's sexual orientation, gay or non-gay, is irrelevant to that parent's ability to raise a child. In addition to the APA, these groups include the American Academy of Family Physicians, the American Psychiatric Association, the American Psychoanalytic Association, the Child Welfare League of America, the North American Council on Adoptable Children, the National Education Association, and the National Association of Social Workers, among others.[17]

And in 2002 the American Academy of Pediatrics, the organization representing our nation's kids' doctors, issued a formal policy statement in support of gay parents and their children. The pediatricians noted that gay parents are fit and loving and their kids are doing well, and recommended that the law provide structures of responsibility and support for those families as for others. Since the pediatricians are perhaps the single most authoritative body of experts on the well-being of children, let me quote their position at some length:

> Children deserve to know that their relationship with both of their parents is stable and legally recognized. This applies to all children, whether their parents are of the same or opposite sex. The American Academy of Pediatrics recognizes that a considerable body of professional literature provides evidence that children with parents who are homosexual can have the same advantages and the same expectations for health, adjustment, and development as can children whose parents are heterosexual. When two adults participate in parenting a child, they and the child deserve the serenity that comes with legal recognition.

Children born or adopted into families headed by partners who are of the same sex usually have only one biological or adoptive legal parent. The other partner in a parental role is called the "co-parent" or "second parent." Because these families and children need the permanence and security that are provided by having two fully sanctioned and legally defined parents, the Academy supports the legal adoption of children by co-parents or second parents. Denying legal parent status through adoption to co-parents or second parents prevents these children from enjoying the psychological and legal security that comes from having two willing, capable, and loving parents.

Several states have considered or enacted legislation sanctioning second-parent adoption by partners of the same sex. In addition, legislative initiatives assuring legal status equivalent to marriage for gay and lesbian partners, such as the law approving civil unions in Vermont, can also attend to providing security and permanence for the children of those partnerships.[18]

In sum, all of the nation's leading organizations for children's health, children's welfare, and mental health have made clear that anti-gay groups, politicians, and commentators are just plain wrong on this important question. When it comes to a child's well-being, what counts is the quality of the parenting and the support provided, not the parent's gay or non-gay sexual orientation. There certainly are some bad gay and lesbian parents out there—just as there are some awful heterosexual parents—but kids, on average, grow up as healthy, as happy, and as well-adjusted when they have the love and support of their two parents of the same sex as the kids who grow up with the same amount of love and support from parents of different sexes. What really makes a difference is a parent's commitment to the child and the resources that parent has to devote to the child's upbringing, whether those resources come in the form of financial support, legal support, social acknowledgment, or the helping hand of a spouse or others.

The anti-gay agenda of politicians like Governor Jeb Bush, right-wing activists like Brian Brown, and opposition commentators like Maggie Gallagher not only flies in the face of abundant and unrefuted research, it seeks to pressure government into passing laws that actually undermine gay parents' ability and deprive them of resources to provide the best for their children.

Think about that for a moment. Even if it were true that different-sex parents are "better" than parents of the same sex—kind of an irrelevant question for the kids who, like it or not, have the parents they have—does it make any sense to punish the kids who are already being raised by the "less good" or the "wrong" parents?

Marriage protects the best interests of children by providing an economic safety net to their families and to the kids themselves, but the kids of gay parents are denied these needed protections. Some examples of the way kids benefit when their parents are free to marry:

♦ The children have automatic and undisputed access to the resources, benefits, and entitlements of both parents.

♦ Married couples do not have to incur any expenses, legal or otherwise, to ensure that both parents have the right to make important medical decisions for their children in case of emergency.

♦ The children of legally married couples are automatically eligible for health coverage and have legal rights through both parents, as well as child support and visitation from both parents in the event of separation.

♦ If one of the parents in a marriage dies, the law provides financial security not only for the surviving spouse, but for the

children as well, by ensuring eligibility for all appropriate entitlements, such as Social Security survivor benefits, and inheritance rights.

◆ Children benefit from the streamlined adoption processes in
marriage that create legal ties between them and both their parents, giving the children legal rights and security.

◆ Kids get the intangible as well as tangible benefits of the family stability and social approval that often accompany marriage.

This safety net is critical for all children, and particularly for kids
growing up in families of lesser means. Politicians opposing marriage equality deny the children of same-sex couples this support.
These real kids are harmed when their parents are denied access to
all the rights and entitlements that can promote their economic
well-being. The children and their families are deprived of protection in case of death, disability, divorce, or other life-changing
events. As Michael Wald's Stanford report concluded, because of
marriage discrimination against gay people, "the children living
with same-sex partners are made to suffer."

A conservative estimate derived from the census is that there
are at least a million kids being raised by gay and lesbian parents in
this country; experts calculate the true number as between 6 million
and 10 million.[19] And because the desire to have and care for children is such a strong one and by no means confined to non-gay
people, that number will only continue to grow. These kids are
not pawns to be discarded in the pursuit of some abstract "better"
family model. They are harmed by the right wing's campaign to
perpetuate their parents' exclusion from marriage. These kids' families are denied the structure, security, and protections—tangible
and intangible—that other families have.

All children have a better chance when they have financial support from both of their parents. And, most importantly, all children

deserve to know that their family is worthy of respect in the eyes of the law. Those protections, that security, that support, and that respect come with the freedom to marry.

* * *

But I suspect that, for some people, there is another level of discomfort that they are wrestling with in coming to terms with the idea of ending marriage discrimination. It's a subliminal fear that goes beyond some of the questions already addressed in this chapter, beyond how married gay parents will directly affect a child's upbringing.

Sometimes when fair-minded people consider marriage equality for the first time they grapple with the desire to do what is right and just and also with their unexamined gut instinct of "how things just are." They think back to their own childhood in a time when marriage equality for same-sex couples and, indeed, the existence of gay people and the reality of our lives were not discussed. Some have a gnawing, often unacknowledged concern that ending discrimination against gay people might somehow affect their own kids' sexual orientation—that standing up for equality might make it more likely that their children will be gay.

It's worth getting this anxiety out in the open and talking about it candidly.

No less a "knee-jerk liberal" than Ronald Reagan actually addressed this concern in 1978, when he spoke out against the Briggs Initiative, a California ballot question that would have prohibited gay men and lesbians from teaching in the state's public schools because of the claim that gay people are "immoral" or bad "role models" who might influence children's sexual orientation. Long silent on the issue of gay rights, the former governor and future president essentially sealed the anti-gay measure's defeat when he spoke out against it. "As to the 'role model' argument, a woman writing to the former editor of a Southern California newspaper said it all," Reagan wrote in an op-ed. " 'If teachers had such power over children I would have been a nun years ago.' " [20]

Likewise, kids today won't turn out to be gay or lesbian just because their parents or teachers are gay, or because they're growing up in a society that is increasingly accepting and supportive of gay people and gay families. While science still hasn't fully determined how our sexual orientation—heterosexual, homosexual, or bisexual—is formed, it's pretty clear that for most people, it is neither a matter of casual choice nor imparted by a parent or role model. Non-gay couples like my happily married parents have children who grow up to be gay like me, just as most of the children raised by gay and lesbian couples grow up to be heterosexual.

Instead of worrying about a conjectural negative message that marriage equality might send to children, consider the opposite concern. What message does it send kids when all they hear about gay people are stories of hardship and hostility?

When some parents consider the possibility that their sons or daughters may grow up to be gay, they talk about the disappointment that would accompany such news. "If Mary were a lesbian she would never be able to have a family," they say. "If Pedro turned out to be gay, he would spend his life alone and we would never have grandchildren." Indeed, most gay and lesbian adults recall having similar worries when they first realized they were gay. Remember the story of how I told my mom, even before I realized that I was gay, that I didn't think I was ever going to be married? I knew as a child that I was just somehow different from what was considered "normal," and thought, even as a child, that the difference was probably enough to count me out of institutions, traditions, and rites that most people have to look forward to in adulthood.

Gay kids are still getting this message loud and clear. Realizing that you might not live up to your parents' expectations, the fear of being left out of so much of what society deems important in adulthood, and the specter of living a life alone and without a family of your own—it's enough for many kids to take pretty drastic actions when they first realize that they might be gay. According to some estimates, gay youth denied support and acceptance are five times as likely to attempt suicide as non-gay youth.[21] For some kids, the prospect of life as a gay adult often seems so challenging, the fear of rejection by their own family seems so daunting, that death looks like a better alternative.

Hostility toward gay men and lesbians sends non-gay kids a message, too. Tolerating discrimination against gay people gives some children a false sense of superiority and tells them it's okay to look down on people who are different. Few parents want to teach their children to despise minorities or people who are different from them. Most realize that teaching kids to hate or disparage others sets their children up for a rocky time in a diverse world, or even worse, can lead them to violence and actions that harm others as well as themselves.

Anti-gay prejudice also puts a burden on non-gay kids to do anything and everything they can to avoid being characterized as different or gay. It pushes kids to conform to crude and restrictive stereotypes and gender roles that limit their own sense of self and sometimes warp their treatment of those of the other sex. Consider the story of Marcus Wayman, an eighteen-year-old high school football player from Minersville, Pennsylvania, who was out with a seventeen-year-old male friend of his in the spring of 1997 when they were both arrested for underage drinking. According to the testimony of Marcus's friend Matthew Adamick, police found condoms in one of the boy's pockets, assumed they were gay, and said to

Marcus, "Your buddy said you're gay." Marcus, who had a girl-friend, told Matthew that he was going to kill himself. Six hours later he took a .44 Magnum handgun and fired it toward his face. When the first shot missed, he fired again, killing himself as he had told Matthew he would.[22]

During the trial of the police officers involved in the case, Marcus's friends testified repeatedly that he was not gay. It is, of course, conceivable that they were wrong and unaware of the pressures Marcus may have been dealing with and felt he could not share—I have no way of knowing. But assuming, as his friends and family believe, that he was not gay, Marcus's terrible ordeal is an example of a young man who was so afraid of the prospect of people thinking he *might* be gay, that death seemed to be a better alternative. "What a lot of straight people don't understand is why someone who is straight would kill himself because he is getting accused of being gay," Marcus's mother, Madonna Sterling, later said. "What we've come to understand, in talking to gay men, is how difficult a decision it is to come out, or to be forced to come out."[23]

Marcus never knew that it wouldn't have mattered to his family what his sexual orientation was—"as long as he was safe and happy," his stepfather, Mark Sterling, said.[24] His parents never had, or never took, the opportunity to let their son know that they loved him unconditionally and would have stood by him and stood up for him because of that love, whether he was gay or not.

If you think about it, that's the message of marriage equality. Gay or non-gay, what matters to those who love you is that you are safe and happy, and have the ability to build a life, contribute to society, dream of a commitment to a partner and a family, and share in the same rights and responsibilities as every other American.

Imagine how different things will be when that message finally gets out—while at the same time most things will not change. Non-gay children won't turn gay or decide on a whim to marry someone of the same sex. It's not like they'll decide, as in the old commercials, that they "could have had a V-8." Families will still be free to teach their own diverse religious beliefs and to raise their children with the values they hold, values that for most parents, gay and non-gay, include fairness, respect, compassion, personal integrity, and doing unto others as you would have them do unto you.

But gay and non-gay alike, children will come to learn—as they already are coming to learn—what is true: that the world includes moms who are lesbian and dads who are gay. They will see happy gay people getting married. They'll see married gay people forming families. They'll see classmates whose parents are now legally married and better able to care for them. They'll see responsibilities and personal commitment as the key to marriage, and government keeping its promise to treat everyone equally under the law.

America has gone through periods of change before that caused people to feel anxious, but fortunately most of us want to do the right thing for our kids as well as for the others with whom we share this time on earth. Think about what the pediatricians, professionals, and scholars have reported. Look at the experience of Canada and other countries, where thousands of couples—including little Robbie Barnett-Kemper's moms—are now legally married and no one has been harmed.[25] Remember that young people are today much more aware of the reality of gay people's lives and are correspondingly less encumbered by the stereotypes and prejudices that earlier generations grew up with. Virtually every poll shows that younger Americans, no matter where they live, no matter what their religious upbringing, overwhelmingly support ending marriage discrimination.[26]

Yes, parents, gay or non-gay—and loving uncles like me—of course want the best for, and have many worries about, our kids. But the inclusion of committed couples in marriage is not one of the things that need worry us.

CHAPTER SIX

ISN'T MARRIAGE

A RELIGIOUS MATTER?

*The traditional family is under attack. I do not know that
things were worse in the times of Sodom and Gomorrah.*
    Mormon Church President Gordon B. Hinckley (2004) [1]

*I believe in an America that is officially neither Catholic,
Protestant, nor Jewish—where no public official either requests or accepts instructions on public policy from the pope,
the National Council of Churches, or any other ecclesiastical
source—where no religious body seeks to impose its will directly or indirectly upon the general populace or the public
acts of its officials—and where religious liberty is so indivisible that an act against one church is treated as an act
against all.*
                          John F. Kennedy (1960) [2]

When many people hear the word *marriage,* the image that may come to mind is a church, synagogue, mosque, or temple full of dressed-up family members and friends. Everyone is glowing with nervous anticipation as they crane their necks and look over their shoulders to see if it's time to stand up for the bride. She, of course, is dressed in a white gown—probably something with lace—and is carrying a bouquet. And when it's finally time for her to march down the aisle, a crescendo of oohs, aahs, and sniffles accompanies each step she takes toward her intended spouse and the religious officiant, who will preside over the ceremony.

It's a beautiful and significant occasion, and undoubtedly it's an event that everyone in attendance will remember for many years to come. Yet, in the eyes of the government, it doesn't mean a thing.

That's because our country is based on a foundation of religious freedom. The First Amendment to our Constitution provides that "Congress shall make no law respecting an establishment of religion, or prohibiting the free exercise thereof." In terms of marriage, this means that, for government purposes, what matters are not the long-planned, beautiful, and memorable religious ceremonies that are a part of many couples' weddings, but the legal papers those couples sign before and afterward. As joyous, spiritual, and important as the religious *rites* of marriage are for many couples, in our country the *right* to marry is, first and foremost, a legal matter that may or may not be witnessed by a religious officiant or celebrated by a religious ceremony, or performed by a judge or clerk in a civil ceremony, as the couple chooses.

It's a careful balance set up by our nation's founders to protect the rights of all citizens to worship—or not worship—as they see fit for themselves. And as the Reverend William G. Sinkford of the Unitarian Universalist Association of Congregations explained in February 2004, opening the doors of marriage to gay and lesbian couples is not going to change this. "Religious marriage will justly remain the prerogative of the individual faith community in accordance with their beliefs. And this is as it should be," Sinkford said. "But the task of our government and elected representatives is not to enshrine in our laws the religious point of view of any one faith; the role of our government is to dedicate itself to protecting the rights of all citizens."[3]

As you've already seen in this book, many opponents of the freedom to marry claim their opposition rests on religious grounds. In a twelve-page document signed by Pope John Paul II's chief theological adviser, Cardinal Joseph Ratzinger, in July 2003, the Vatican stated, "There are absolutely no grounds for considering homosexual unions to be in any way similar or even remotely analogous to God's plan for marriage and family. . . . Marriage is holy, while homosexual acts go against the natural moral law."[4]

Just a couple of weeks later, Elder Russell M. Ballard, a member of the Mormon Church's Quorum of the Twelve, told a group in Provo, Utah, that allowing gay couples to marry would threaten God's plan for children here and in eternity. The church "must stand firm at this time when the adversary is using differing lifestyles in an attempt to replace the sanctity of marriage between one man and one woman."[5]

And after the Massachusetts Supreme Judicial Court ruled against marriage discrimination, Rabbi Chaim Schwartz of the Orthodox Jewish advocacy coalition Agudath Israel of New England made a "slippery slope" argument against equality. "It's not that we do not believe in the civil rights of gay couples—we believe each person should be able to live in this great country—but we don't believe in calling it marriage," Schwartz said. "It's morally incorrect, and what's next? Bestiality? Marrying a dog? Marrying your cat?"[6]

As loud as our opponents have been, many people might not realize that religions actually differ on this issue. For example, hundreds of religious leaders in Massachusetts, from Baptists to Buddhists and from Episcopalians to Jews, have signed that state's "Declaration of Religious Support for the Freedom of Same-Gender Couples to Marry." The Union of American Hebrew Congregations, the Central Conference of American Rabbis, the Unitarian Universalist Association, and other denominations have spoken in support of civil-marriage equality. But as the Reverend Peter Gomes of Harvard University's Memorial Church explained in a speech at the Massachusetts Statehouse, "Religious views in these constitutional matters—no matter how deeply felt—are irrelevant."

If any clergy "wish to address within their considerable constituencies the problems and opportunities of marriage, as they say, by all means, and with God's grace, let them do so," Gomes said. "Surely, if they do in fact represent thousands of believers, there must be thousands of opportunities for them to define and defend marriage by the light of their traditions. Their failures or inability to do so should not be transferred to the backs of either the civil law or the civil rights of homosexuals."[7]

Indeed, there are many church leaders who don't support marriage equality but, because they revere the separation of church and state, do respect the boundaries between what they preach on Sundays and what they would have the law impose by force. "Though the church, and though I, have firm convictions about sexuality, our ministry is primarily about people's spiritual life and not about pushing a political agenda," explained Jeff Manion, pastor of the evangelical Ada Bible Church in Ada, Michigan.[8] Others, such as Bishop Susan Hassinger, the top United Methodist Church official in New England, told parishioners that in current Methodist doctrine "the covenant of marriage is reserved for heterosexual couples," but also pointed out that the church's Social Principles explicitly promote "basic human rights . . . for homosexual persons" and therefore "imply support" for court decisions in favor of those legal rights.[9]

The freedom-to-marry movement isn't about forcing any religious institution—whether it supports marriage equality or opposes it—to change any of its views or tenets on this question or any other. This civil rights movement is about equal legal *rights,* not diverse religious *rites.* And because civil marriage licenses are obtained from the government, ending sex discrimination in legal or "civil" marriage won't compel any change in our nation's churches, synagogues, mosques, and temples. Even after government opens the doors to marriage equality, it can't and won't force religious institutions to open their doors to perform those marriages. The Vatican won't have to order its priests to marry gay or lesbian couples in its cathedrals, just as priests do not have to celebrate the second or third marriages of divorced Catholics (who, despite their church's views, are allowed to get civil marriage licenses and remarry outside the church). Mormons won't be compelled to change their temple ceremonies to accommodate same-sex couples, any more than they have to marry Jewish couples. And Orthodox Jews won't need to welcome two brides or two grooms (or dogs or cats, for that matter) under the *chupa.*

The strength of our nation's constitutional commitment to religious freedom is dependent upon the equally important principle that no religion or religious institution gets to impose its own dictates on the government. In other words, for church and state to remain separate, as most Americans agree they should, we must do as

Jesus suggested and "render unto Caesar what is Caesar's and render unto God what is God's." [10] Religious institutions, under the direction of their individual leaders and religious teachings, preach what they believe is best for those people who share the same faith, while we all respect the right of every American to hold differing faiths and beliefs equally under the law. Government should not be a weapon used to impose religious rules or parochial interpretations on others.

"We respect the right of the Catholic Church to set its own policies and its own definition of marriage, but the Catholic Church does not have the right to impose its religious beliefs on others," said Rabbi Devon A. Lerner, one of the 400-plus clergy who make up the Religious Coalition for the Freedom to Marry. "Equal civil marriage will not force priests, or any clergy, to change their beliefs or practices—our laws of separation of church and state guarantee that." [11]

Divorce law provides a good example of how this line between church and the government works when it comes to marriage. As far as the Catholic Church is concerned, marriage is one of seven sacraments—the others being baptism, confirmation, eucharist, penance, anointing of the sick, and holy orders—and is indissoluble until death. Obviously churches differ over what is a sacrament, or what a sacrament means, or whether they have sacraments at all, as is their right. Given its particular doctrines on sacraments and marriage as a union for life, the Catholic Church does not condone remarriage after divorce, nor does it recognize divorces issued by other institutions. Nevertheless, it's been a long time since even the most extreme Catholic leader in the U.S. has suggested that government should not issue marriage licenses to divorced couples (or even to divorced Catholic couples). Imagine some of the couples who would have been prevented from marrying if such a religious standard were imposed upon civil law in America (as it has been in other countries, many of which are now moving to allow civil divorce over church opposition there): Ronald and Nancy Reagan, John and Cindy McCain, and John Kerry and Teresa Heinz Kerry, to name a few.

Similarly, many rabbis interpret Jewish law to hold that a rabbi can only preside over the wedding of a Jewish couple. Of course, even though civil law allows for interfaith couples to marry, no rabbi can be forced to perform such a marriage. And, in fact, there are other rabbis who believe that blessing an interfaith couple is perfectly permissible, based on that couple's commitment and Jewish values; the law's neutrality allows those rabbis and couples to make their own decisions, too.

This distinctively American constitutional balance only works when the "wall of separation," as Thomas Jefferson described it, between church and state is respected and kept clear. A willful blurring of the line between religious rites and the legal right to marry is an assault on the very religious freedom that is one of this country's greatest gifts to the rest of the world, a gift that makes the very idea of pluralism possible. When President Bush threw his political weight behind a proposed amendment to the U.S. Constitution that would block gay couples from what he characterized as the "sacred institution" of marriage, he not only attacked gay people, he also misleadingly conflated religious marriage and legal marriage. He ignored the important fact that *with regard to the government's role* (and the oath Bush took as president), marriage is a legal, not sacred, institution. In America, we don't look to government to regulate or issue licenses for sacred or religious ceremonies or institutions; we don't elect presidents or trust to politicians to govern "sanctity" or decide whether there are sacraments or what should be done about them. That would be dangerous to the American idea of religious freedom that respects us as individuals, protects our nation's churches and synagogues, and helps keep our pluralistic nation united, not divided.

Nearly 40 percent of marriages in the United States take place without any religious ceremony, in civil ceremonies presided over by judges, clerks, justices of the peace, or even, for some non-gay couples in Las Vegas, Elvis impersonators. Just as Americans are free to disagree over religious matters and still be equal under the law, so are couples who choose to have civil ceremonies to mark their marriage free to do so. As long as the legal criteria and responsibilities are met, they are married.

Moreover, religions disagree among themselves when it comes to what President Bush likes to call the "sanctity" of marriage, neglecting to draw the legal distinction between rites and rights. As mentioned, the Catholic Church, for example, now considers marriage a sacrament while the Jewish and Muslim faiths and many Protestant denominations do not. While it is true that many consider marriage to have sanctity, and their views are worthy of respect, it is not up to government to decide who is "right"; each faith decides these questions for itself, while government looks to the equality of all.

The president's failure to comprehend, or his political decision to ignore, this basic American principle underscores why we as Americans revere the separation of church and state—and how each generation is called upon to defend that American gift to the world. Our generation's duty is to end discrimination in marriage.

Unfortunately, the president is not the only one blurring the line. Several religious leaders are doing so as well. The Mormon Church, which gave millions of dollars to anti-gay-marriage campaigns in Hawaii and Alaska, urged church members in California to give their "means and time" to support California's Proposition 22, which in 2000 mandated discrimination against same-sex couples married in other states by barring legal acknowledgment of their marriages. In a May 1999 letter read at more than one thousand Mormon stake houses throughout California, Mormon Church president Gordon B. Hinckley said the issue "lies at the heart of the Lord's eternal plan for his children" and that "the divinely established institution of marriage will be protected as we vote yes."[12] Hinckley's letter urging imposition of the Mormon theological perspective on California law was so successful that it raised a good portion of the $8 million spent by the anti-gay campaign—not to mention questions about the Mormon Church's tax-exempt status.[13]

Meanwhile, the Catholic Church, which itself gave close to half a million dollars to push for the anti-gay California proposition, is now setting its sights on an anti-gay constitutional amendment in Massachusetts. Though the church hierarchy is in crisis over its failure to prevent—and its role in covering up—decades of child abuse, and even as the church has had to close schools and cut back on services, the state's four bishops found the time and resources to send a mailing to one million households urging them to fight marriage equality, and the Massachusetts Catholic Conference sent priests an anti-gay video, which was shown during Sunday services.[14] "Sadly, in recent years, we have witnessed the breakdown of family life in Western society due to no-fault divorce and generalization of the acceptance of cohabitation," said Archbishop Sean P. O'Malley of Boston.[15] (Of course neither the archbishop nor the Massachusetts Catholic Conference has thereby chosen to press for a constitutional amendment to restrict divorce or bar couples from living together, which would apply to all Americans, but rather they aim their fire only at gay couples seeking equality in marriage.)

In 2003, the U.S. Conference of Catholic Bishops issued not

one, but two statements attacking gay couples' desire to marry, and threw in a condemnation of contraception as well (though, again, when it comes to action, they only call for a constitutional amendment aimed at gay people). Under the headline "The People Are Watching," a church newspaper demanded that Catholics contact their legislators to vote for an anti-gay constitutional amendment.[16] The Catholic Action League called for the impeachment of the four Massachusetts high court justices who ruled in favor of marriage equality, saying that they "violated their oath, made a mockery of the separation of powers, and usurped the right of the people and their elected representatives."[17]

And what if basic civil rights were put to a popular vote, as the Catholic Action League also demands?

Harvard's Reverend Gomes, the African-American clergyman who spoke so eloquently at the Massachusetts Statehouse about the importance of the separation between church and state, also warned against throwing the civil rights of a minority to a vote. "The danger in the seemingly 'democratic' process of the popular vote is that the principle of inalienable human rights is now subject to the actions of the majority; we are a nation of laws, and not of referenda at the fundamental level of human and civil rights. Our whole constitutional history has been the enlargement of rights, not their restriction," he told state senators in February 2004.

"Suppose a referendum was the instrument used by an Anglo-Saxon Protestant majority to define in law the social and legal position of Irish Catholics? This statehouse and commonwealth would look and feel very differently than it does today," Gomes said.

Suppose a referendum was the instrument used by a white slaveholding majority in the old South to define the social and legal position of African-Americans? Well, they did, and we know the answer to that hypothetical. . . . And what of Mormons, Jews, and any other minority subject to the legislative whim of a well-organized majority designed to consecrate the status quo? Consequences: As our court has opined as recently as last week: "Separate is hardly ever equal." [18]

Indeed, as Gomes pointed out, religion and the government haven't always seen eye to eye when it comes to civil rights. That was the case with slavery, when many churches defended that institution even after the Civil War, invoking the many biblical passages that encourage and regulate slavery, such as this set of instructions from Leviticus: "[Y]ou may purchase male or female slaves from among the foreigners who live among you. You may also purchase the children of such resident foreigners, including those who have been born in your land. You may treat them as your property, passing them on to your children as a permanent inheritance." [19]

From today's vantage point, with our values, we see that religion has often been on the wrong side regarding the subordination of women, and interracial marriage as well. Many religions, like government and other pillars of society, struggled with and resisted racial equality and women's equality for a long time, defending inequality as divinely ordained and part of the natural order of things, the very definition of how life was meant to be. Many churches have changed for the better, but some are still struggling.

History tells us that some "catch-up" time may well be okay under our Constitution; the American system allows for debate, divergence, and state-by-state differences, and courts and legislatures all have their say and play their part. But history also underscores the point made so powerfully by President Kennedy, that no religious body should seek to "impose its will directly or indirectly upon the general populace or the public acts of its officials," just as religious liberty should be "so indivisible that an act against one church is treated as an act against all."

Certainly if we follow Kennedy's words and the Constitution's command, no religious body will be—or should feel—threatened by an end to government discrimination in marriage. That said, if you still find yourself with a hesitation regarding the freedom to marry that you believe is based in your religious beliefs, I encourage you to examine the roots of that discomfort more deeply.

If you're like most people, there have been many times when you've come up against choices in life that contradict your religion's doctrine. And in those cases, there have certainly been times when you thought things through for yourself, when you decided as a matter of conscience and judgment which part of the doctrine was appropriate for your life and which part of it was not.

For example, most Catholics use birth control, even though the Vatican is vehemently against it, and even more Catholics oppose the Vatican's telling American lawmakers that they should restrict all people's ability to decide for themselves whether or not to use contraception, a matter of choice under the law and Constitution. Pope John Paul II came out against the war in Iraq, while, at least initially, the majority of Americans (and many Catholic politicians) supported President Bush's choice to send in the troops. And even though a good number of religions are opposed to the death penalty, the president has not talked about the sanctity of life in that context.

Few people walk in complete lockstep with even their own faith's view of how they should live their lives, and even fewer believe that we should use our government as a weapon to impose religious choices on our fellow Americans. So why should the law of marriage—that is, marriage under the law—or equality for gay people be handled any differently?

If you have concerns about ending marriage discrimination based on interpretations of what the Bible says, I encourage you to take another look at that, too. And before we turn to the biblical passages and interpretations, let's remember, each religion has its differing sources and texts; not every faith shares the same creed or bible, and even those who appeal to what most of us call "the" Bible have different versions—Catholic, varied Protestant, varied Jewish—and different interpretations of that set of scriptures.

Episcopal Bishop John Shelby Spong has written that most people who claim to be compelled to support discrimination because of the Bible's alleged condemnation of gay people invoke one of seven passages. Three of those passages—all of them in the New Testament—are not even about gay people, the Bishop notes. They "appear to refer to sexual anomalies such as temple prostitution, pederasty, or forced sexual activity, which are quite unrelated to homosexuality."[20] Why the misplaced emphasis on these misunderstood fragments? Bishop Spong and others ask.

Let's look at the other four passages a bit more closely. The first, from the book of Genesis, is perhaps the best known and most often misinterpreted. It is the story of God's punishment of the towns of Sodom and Gomorrah, and often is invoked to label homosexuality as sinful and the cause of God's wrath. The Bible says that two angels visit the town of Sodom disguised as humans. The strangers are threatened by the townspeople and Abraham's nephew, Lot, finally offers them refuge. When the townspeople come to take the visitors by force, Lot, in an effort to calm the mounting mob, offers to let them rape his two virgin daughters rather than surrender the visitors. Later Lot himself has sex with the same daughters and impregnates them. "I never hear this narrative quoted to affirm incest," the bishop writes. "Yet this strange biblical passage continues to be used to condemn homosexuality. Perhaps those who quote it in this manner might want to read the whole story." [21]

Spong, like many religious leaders and most modern scholars, understands the story of God's destruction of Sodom to be about hospitality and the proper treatment of strangers, and not at all about gay people, let alone the civil rights of same-sex couples. In fact, the Bible itself says that the Sodom story is not about singling out gay people for discrimination, or even about sex. For example, Ezekiel 16:48–49 explains, "Behold this was the iniquity of thy sister Sodom, pride, fullness of bread, and abundance of idleness was in her and her daughters, neither did she strengthen the hand of the poor and the needy." This and other biblical passages make clear that the arrogant disregard of the equal human needs of others is what brought Sodom down—a context and lesson not often shared by the anti-gay forces who invoke religion to impose their own political agenda.

Indeed, in some faith traditions, there is an even deeper lesson to the oft-misused Sodom story. As one Jewish commentator sums it up, "The sin of Sodom consisted not only in what its people did, but in what they failed to do. . . . Failure to protest is to participate in the sin of a community." [22]

The next two passages sometimes invoked against gay people come from Leviticus, which is also part of what Jews call the Torah and Christians call the Old Testament. The passages are found in Leviticus's "Holiness Code," prohibited acts of "uncleanness" designed to instruct the Children of Israel on how to distinguish themselves from others. Amidst a litany of prohibitions, Leviticus 18:22 condemns a man "who lies with a male as with a woman," and the second passage a little later orders the death penalty for this and many other acts. [23] Varying interpretations have been offered of the Leviticus passages, which are phrased more ambiguously than many translations make out; some interpretations emphasize that what was prohibited was only male-male sex or only a certain kind of penetration, while others note that at that time in history women were subordinated to men—lamentably, even within the Bible itself—and thus to "lie with a man as with a woman" would be to "diminish" him or, at least, fail to embrace the distinctiveness and equal goodness of same-sex relationships.[24]

Regardless of how one reads these passages, however, the same book of Leviticus condemns, and orders the same punishment for, adultery, eating seafood without fins, getting a tattoo, or wearing clothes made out of two different fabrics.[25] And, as Bishop Spong points out, the Bible also calls for the death penalty for those who worship a false god and for children who talk back to their parents.

As mentioned earlier, Leviticus also says, as did religious leaders right through the Civil War, that slavery is a legitimate trade. Several American denominations such as the Southern Baptists owe their existence to institutional schisms that occurred when leaders and congregations refused to abandon their faith-based support of slavery.[26] As we've seen, Leviticus gives meticulous instructions regarding whom it is okay to enslave (generally those not of the faith), but at the same time, reminds the Children of Israel, themselves former slaves, "When a stranger resides with you in your land, you shall not wrong him. The stranger who resides with you shall be to you as one of your citizens; you shall love him as yourself, for you were strangers in the land of Egypt."[27] Clearly some picking and choosing is required—and every religion does so.

The last passage invoked to justify anti-gay sentiments is from the New Testament and, according to Spong, is the quirkiest of them all. In Romans 1:27, it seems as if Paul says that God will punish people who do not worship properly, by confusing their sexual identities so that men sleep with men and women sleep with women. "What a strange God!" the bishop exclaims. "Thus saith the Lord; 'If you don't worship me properly I will turn you into gays and lesbians.' I have a hard time imagining anyone worshipping such a capricious and egocentric deity."[28]

The Bible has not always been the clearest of guides, concludes Spong; we all must and do bring something to it. Biblical passages

> had to be proved wrong before the divine right of kings could be pushed aside and the Magna Carta accepted. [They] had to be defeated before Galileo's ideas about the non-centrality of this planet in the universe could usher in the world of astronomy, and before Darwin's understanding of evolution could win the day. The clear teaching of the Bible also had to be overcome before slavery and segregation could be ended and before women could escape their second-class status.[29]

Clearly there are biblical passages that people choose to follow literally, and there are others we recognize as having been written thousands of years ago and, since times and society have changed, we realize they are no longer specifically and literally reflective of the values and understanding with which we live our lives and govern our society today. As the Reverend John Buehrens has written, "the scriptures should be available to everyone, so that all might claim their powers of *interpretation* and understanding."[30] Buehrens quotes Ralph Waldo Emerson—"God speaketh, not spake"—and counsels that we all must, and all do, exercise conscience and judgment, and make choices.[31]

* * *

If after considering all of this, you realize that any discomfort you may have about gay people or with marriage equality is based less in religion and more in a "that's just the way things are done" sense of tradition, ask yourself another question: "Is discomfort, or a vague sense of that's the way we're used to, a good enough reason for government to continue discriminating in a manner harmful to others?"

Imagine, for example, that the U.S. Constitution were amended to embody a literal interpretation of what the Bible says about marriage. In February 2004, U.S. Representative Jim McDermott of Washington state placed into the *Congressional Record* a widely circulated e-mail that described what such a Federal Biblical Marriage Amendment might look like:

> Marriage shall consist of a union between one man and one *or more* women. That is from Genesis 29:17–28.
>
> Secondly, marriage shall not impede a man's right to take concubines in addition to his wife or wives. That is II Samuel 5:13 and II Chronicles 11:21.
>
> A marriage shall be considered valid only if the wife is a virgin. If the wife is not a virgin, she shall be executed. That is Deuteronomy 22:13.
>
> Marriage of a believer and a nonbeliever shall be forbidden. That is Genesis 24:3.
>
> Finally, it says that since there is no law that can change things, divorce is not possible, and finally, if a married man dies, his brother has to marry his sister-in-law.[32]

During the March 2004 debate in the Massachusetts Legislature over whether to amend the state constitution so as to deny gay couples the right to marry, Senator Marian Walsh candidly "admitted that the concept of gay marriage was a bit outside her comfort zone."[33] Nevertheless, she voted against putting discrimination into the constitution, a "particularly courageous" act of principle, said the *Boston Globe,* "given her conservative district and Catholic background." Walsh explained that the high court decision in *Goodridge* "is ahead of our mainstream culture and my own sensibilities [but] my level of comfort is not the appropriate monitor of the Constitutional rights of my constituents. . . . [The Constitution] has always required us to reach beyond our moral and emotional grasp."[34]

In this chapter, I have included many references to various religious stances and biblical passages, but my aim is not to try to change anyone's religious beliefs. I don't here suggest that people have to agree with Bishops Sinkford or Spong, Reverends Gomes or Buehrens, the Central Conference of American Rabbis, or the many other religious leaders who support legal marriage equality. Readers need not adopt any particular version or interpretation of religious texts, and for that matter, they may have no religious views on the subject at all.

Rather I want to illustrate a different point: As Americans we are free—preciously free—to disagree in our faiths and still be treated equally under the law.

The good news here is that we can end discrimination in marriage—end the denial of the right to marry for committed same-sex couples willing to take on the rules and responsibilities set forth in the law of marriage—without impairing or harming anyone's freedom of religion. We can all make religious choices in our life while respecting our fellow citizens' equality under the law.

In cautioning Americans against religious self-righteousness, Abraham Lincoln long ago noted that during the Civil War, "Both [sides] read the same Bible, and pray to the same God; and each invokes his aid against the other." Lincoln, a man of immense moral character and vision, urged his fellow countrymen, us, both to act "[w]ith malice toward none, with charity toward all, with firmness in the right, as God gives us to see the right" and to "let us judge not that we be not judged." [35]

While our government sticks to the shared, secular "sacred" text of equality and freedom that is our Constitution, leaving it to each faith to preach its own texts and leaving it to each of us to choose our own diverse religious views, perhaps one phrase from the Bible that all of us as Americans can agree to follow is the one engraved on our Liberty Bell: "Proclaim liberty throughout all the land unto *all* the inhabitants thereof." [36]

CHAPTER SEVEN

WHY NOT USE
ANOTHER WORD?

Some say let's choose another route and give gay folks some legal rights but call it something other than marriage. We have been down that road before in this country. Separate is not equal. The rights to liberty and happiness belong to each of us and on the same terms, without regard to either skin color or sexual orientation.

Congressman John Lewis (2003)[1]

The dissimilitude between the terms "civil marriage" and "civil union" is not innocuous; it is a considered choice of language that reflects a demonstrable assigning of same-sex, largely homosexual, couples to second-class status.

Opinions of the Justices to the Massachusetts Senate (2004)[2]

Those heterosexuals still uneasy with same-sex marriage often ask, "Why marriage? Why can't you have all the rights and benefits and just call it something else?" Our answer is simple: Because then it would be something else.

Columnist Deb Price (2003)[3]

During the first three months after Vermont's civil-union law went into effect on July 1, 2000, more than 800 couples registered their civil union with the state's health department. And, considering the excitement around the country regarding the groundbreaking, first-of-its kind law, I wasn't too surprised to find out that about 600 of those first civil unions were performed for couples who weren't even from Vermont. Today, more than 5,000 couples have been joined in civil union, over 4,250 of them from out of state.

The new law was a historic step forward at the time. Calling it something other than marriage—"civil union"—the state created a parallel, non-marriage marital status to provide marital responsibilities and rights at the state level to committed gay and lesbian couples in Vermont. Civil unions marked a significant, if incomplete, answer to the prayers of many people around the country eager for legal structure to reinforce and respect their personal commitment to a same-sex life partner.

But if you don't quite understand what a "parallel, non-marriage marital status" is, read on. As you will find, you're not alone.

Susan Burns and Debra Freer of Atlanta, Georgia, were among the hundreds of couples who headed to Vermont in those first few months. The women were issued a civil-union license the day after the law went into effect, and they exchanged vows during a ceremony in the Green Mountains two days later—on the Fourth of July. Aside from the symbolism and personal meaning that their civil union had for the Freers (Susan took Debra's last name after the ceremony), they hoped that it would also give their relationship some much-needed legal currency.

You see, when Susan and her husband, Darian, divorced in 1995, they agreed to a decree regarding visitation of their three children. The agreement forbade visitation by the children "with either parent during any time where such party cohabits with or has overnight stays with any adult to which such party is not legally married or to whom party is not related within the second degree."

Years later, after Susan met Debra and they moved in together, Susan's ex-husband decided to try to cut off Susan's visits with her children. In effect, Georgia's ban on allowing same-sex couples to wed was forcing Susan to choose between the woman she loved and her children. Vermont's civil-union law, though, seemed to offer a lifeline. Even though not a marriage, their civil union was certainly a solemn legal undertaking and a genuine state-certified legal status, a reflection of their commitment to one another, and a binding statement that they had become legally "related" as family and next of kin. Susan and Debra hoped that Georgia would see they had done all they could to create permanence and stability, given the state's marriage discrimination against them, and would at least treat that legal commitment and status with the common sense and compassion that family courts routinely accord other family problems, or even business contracts.

But that hasn't been the case. So far, two Georgia courts have disagreed with Susan and her ACLU lawyers, saying that not only is a civil union not a marriage, but it is essentially a nothing—a legal family status that nevertheless brings no acknowledgment, respect, or legal weight whatsoever in the state of Georgia. Conceding only the catch-22 that the state's marriage discrimination has created for people like Susan Freer—no family protections without marriage, but no marriage for certain families—the appeals court ruled that Georgia's anti-gay "defense of marriage" law, which makes marriage available solely to a man and woman, forbids the court to accord a civil union any respect, whether as a marriage or even just as a marker of familial relationship and commitment. So Susan and other gay parents like her in Georgia are not only barred from getting married, they are also denied recognition when it comes to any other kinds of legal commitments that might otherwise shore up and reflect their family structure and stability.

John Langan and Neal Conrad Spicehandler of Massapequa Park, New York, exchanged rings and legal vows in Vermont four months after the Freers. Their civil union was as much a celebration of the fifteen years they had spent together as it was a testament to the many more years they hoped to be together. A little more than a year later, Conrad was hospitalized after being injured in a hit-and-run accident. While his injuries were serious (he required two surgeries on one of his legs), there wasn't any indication that he wouldn't fully recover. In fact, after three days in the hospital, Conrad's friends and family said he was his old self again as he prepared for his second surgery and what the staff said would be his release within a few days. John, who had spent almost the entire time since the accident by his partner's side, took the opportunity to go home and get some sleep.

Early the next morning, John woke up to a phone call from the hospital saying that Conrad had died. John never got to say goodbye. Instead, he was given the note that Conrad had written on his way into the operating room. It read:

> John:
> I'm going under. I haven't had a chance to see you.
>   I love you.
>   I've made my life in your heart.
>   Conrad[4]

When the hospital was unable to explain to the family's satisfaction how the routine surgery turned fatal, John, along with Conrad's mother, Ruth, sued the hospital for wrongful death and medical malpractice as well as Conrad's pain and suffering. The hospital responded, however, by seeking to get John's part of the case thrown out of court, arguing that John and Conrad's civil union did not qualify John to sue as a spouse under New York law. It took months of legal wrangling, which the grieving John wouldn't have had to endure if he and Conrad had been married, before a judge ruled that he could indeed sue, like other family members, for the loss of his love.

Meanwhile, in Beaumont, Texas, John Anthony and Russell Smith's civil union was less than a year old when the couple decided to call it quits. Russell wanted the divorce to be legal, though, because he wanted to make sure the several business deals he and John had made as a couple were handled appropriately. Recognizing the couple's civil union as the binding undertaking that it is, a district judge granted them a divorce. But when Texas Attorney General Greg Abbott read about the judge's commonsense response, he publicly criticized the decision and made the highly unusual request that the court set it aside. Although neither the state nor the attorney general was a litigant in the case—this divorce was, after all, a family matter—the judge acceded to the attorney general's request and retracted his ruling. John and Russell were forced to separate without the legal guidelines and clarity available to married couples.

People often ask if it wouldn't be better to use a different word than *marriage* in the freedom-to-marry campaign. If you just "call it something else," they conjecture, "you can get all the rights of marriage while placating those who just aren't ready to see gay people get married." When I'm asked this question, I point to examples like Susan and Debra's, John and Conrad's, and John and Russell's. Because Vermont uses a different word than *marriage,* the Freers are denied child visitation rights, John Langan had to fight in court to prove his commitment to his partner of fifteen years, and John and Russell can't get a divorce in their home state.

Couples like these are denied one of the main benefits of marriage: marriage.

As much as I disagree with the politically motivated meddling of the Texas attorney general into John and Russell's family matter, it is true that civil unions are not the same as marriage. Civil unions are separate from and unequal to marriage. Unlike couples who are married in Vermont, couples who are joined in civil unions can't confidently carry the rights and responsibilities bestowed upon them across the state's borders, because no other state has a civil-union law and, for that matter, neither does the federal government. That means many of the thousands of gay couples who travel to Vermont to exchange vows will find no legal recognition of their commitment when they return home. And couples who live in Vermont may be forced to leave their legal family status behind when they travel outside the state, whether to go shopping across the border in New Hampshire or vacationing across the country in Nevada.

I want to be careful here not to discount the importance of what happened in Vermont when three couples—Stan Baker and Peter Harrigan, Nina Beck and Stacy Jolles, and Lois Farnham and Holly Puterbaugh—sued the state for the freedom to marry. It was just three years after Judge Kevin Chang's landmark Hawaii decision that a nearly unanimous Vermont Supreme Court came to a similar conclusion in 1999. The justices said that extending equal rights to gay and lesbian Vermonters "who seek nothing more, nor less, than legal protection and security for their avowed commitment to an intimate and lasting human relationship is simply, when all is said and done, a recognition of our common humanity."[5]

Ruling that Vermont had a "constitutional obligation to extend to [same-sex couples] the common benefit, protection, and security" provided different-sex married couples, the justices nevertheless stopped short of telling the state how to meet that obligation. They instead passed that responsibility—and the buck—to the state legislature.[6]

Of the academics, activists, clergy, lawyers, and others who subsequently presented testimony to the legislature, almost all of them fell into two camps: one saying the court was correct and that full marriage equality should be extended to gay and lesbian couples, and the other saying the court was wrong and that same-sex couples should get no legal protections or acknowledgment.[7] As University of Michigan law professor David Chambers later pointed out, "Almost no one can be heard promoting domestic partnership," or what later came to be called "civil union." Chambers reported, "Those who support traditional marriage say domestic partnership would undermine it. Those who support gay marriage say the state should settle for nothing less."[8]

Nevertheless, the state's lawmakers showed themselves both afraid to stand up for true equality and unwilling to defy the constitution and provide no legal recognition at all. As the political pressures and right-wing opposition ratcheted up, many people who would have preferred equality supported the new concept of civil union as better than nothing, while others on the anti-gay side gave temporary support to the new status as preferable to extending full equal rights to gay people.[9]

In fact, civil unions are unequal—and *are* better than nothing. They have made a very real difference for thousands of American couples. Outside of the tangible benefits for in-state families, there is also no doubt of the law's symbolic significance for couples such as John Langan and Neal Conrad Spicehandler, who lived a committed life together for fifteen years before they ever had the opportunity to undertake a legal commitment to match, declare, and reinforce their love. And for couples such as Susan and Debra Freer, for whom a civil union gave them at least the hope of a legal leg to stand on, civil union seemed the best option available to gay and lesbian couples, at least until California's recently enacted "all-but-marriage" law and, of course, the prospect of full marriage rights in Canada and Massachusetts, which followed later.

In addition, what happened in Vermont, like the engagement in Hawaii, elevated the discussion about marriage equality. Now, when people discuss "gay marriage," even people in the political center increasingly agree that gay people should, at least, have access to an "all-but-marriage" alternative, such as civil unions.

But don't be fooled. It's not as if we have two complete systems of protection in this country with symmetrical gateways, and it's "merely" a matter of non-gay couples entering through the front door and gays going around back. Unlike the institution of marriage, civil union exists in only one state, and civil unions—and any "gay marriage" alternative—are inherently unequal. They are unequal in the security, clarity, and status they provide, unequal in the legal protections that flow from them, unequal in fact as well as in name—and names or words, of course, matter.

Let's take a step back now and look at just what rights civil unions do provide. As we delve deeper, remember that the larger context in the freedom-to-marry movement is ending government's denial of civil marriage licenses and equality in the law of marriage, not interfering with the religious freedom that allows each religion to decide for itself what marriages to perform. Corralling gay couples into a separate and unequal status such as civil unions does nothing to "protect the sanctity" of marriage because the nondiscriminatory issuance of civil marriage licenses does not oblige any religious institution to perform or not perform a religious ceremony.

For 15 percent of the couples who have been issued civil-union licenses—those who live in Vermont—the law provides parallel access to the same three hundred or so rights and responsibilities provided married heterosexual couples directly under state law. These include marital tax status, parenting, divorce, inheritance, family leave, and hospital visitation rights, as well as the responsibility for a partner's debts. But it is at best uncertain how Vermonters joined in civil union will fare if they leave their state, and lovely as Vermont is, people do leave it now and then . . .

What about the rights civil unions don't provide?

Well, first, as we've already mentioned, 85 percent of the couples joined in civil union don't necessarily get any of these legal or economic protections for their families, despite their legal commitment and state-declared spousal status. Why? Because they don't live in Vermont. Unlike marriages performed in Vermont, or any other state in the country, civil unions have no assured portability.

Remember, unlike marriage—good from coast to coast—civil union exists in, yes, only one state. Though civil unions will be honored more and more over time, either piecemeal, incident by incident, or, eventually, as a recognizable status, as part of our nation's overall progress toward marriage equality (recently New York state Attorney General Eliot Spitzer formally noted that the law of that state favors treating out-of-state unions and marriages equally), families should not have to see their legal status and protections sputter in and out like cell-phone service.

Imagine, for example, that your parents were married in their home state but were made legally unmarried when they came to visit you. Aside from being just downright insulting and awkward, it would be tragic if your dad, for whatever reason, had to be hospitalized and your mom wasn't allowed to be with him in the hospital room—or had to produce five forms and see an attorney first—because she wasn't considered his legal next of kin.

Since the federal government won't play ball when it comes to civil unions, couples get none of the IRS, Social Security, Medicare/ Medicaid, or immigration protections that are afforded married couples, to name a few of the 1,138 ways in which federal law makes marriage a factor. Nor are they eligible to take leave from work to care for their loved one.

Carol Moseley Braun, the first and so far only African-American woman elected to the U.S. Senate, answered this way in 2003 when asked her position on marriage versus civil unions: "People should not be discriminated against in the exercise of their civil rights, and the right to marry whom you want to marry is one of those rights. I had an aunt in the 1950s who was married to a German fellow. Their marriage was illegal in half the states. Interracial marriage was regarded with much the same hysteria 100 years ago as gay marriage is today."[10]

She continued:

> If civil unions were to encompass all of the legal rights that marriage does, then I would say, call it a civil union, call it marriage—you can call it "strawberries" for all I care. It doesn't matter. The legal rights are the same. Unfortunately, civil union does not carry with it the same rights as marriage does. For that reason, I say that people in homosexual relationships ought to be able to legitimatize those relationships on the same grounds as people in heterosexual relationships.

The Senator nailed one of the key reasons why "another word" is not the answer: There is no other actual existing legal institution, no legal *system,* apart from marriage, and no other "word" thus brings with it all the actual legal and economic protections and responsibilities our society accords through marriage at the federal, state, and local levels, as well as in the private sector.

And there is another equally important reason why "another word" won't cut it.

As we've discussed throughout this book, there is the ever-important currency of the word *marriage.* When it comes to people's understanding of what it means to be a couple—in love, committed, and responsible to each other—the words *civil union* just can't compare, even if they did somehow pack all the tangible and systemic rights and responsibilities conferred by marriage. As Beth Robinson, who argued the Vermont case in the state supreme court, points out, "nobody writes songs about" civil unions. While everyone knows what you mean when you say "We got married," civil union doesn't even have a verb.

William Safire, who describes himself as a libertarian conservative, or a "libcon," did a good job describing this distinction in his *New York Times* column: "The conservative in me wonders: if equal rights can be assured by civil union, why are some gays pushing so hard for the word 'marriage'?" he wrote in December 2003. "The answer is that the ancient word conveys a powerful message. Civil union connotes toleration of homosexuality, with its attendant recognition of an individual's civil rights; but marriage connotes society's full approval of homosexuality, with previous moral judgment reversed."[11]

That connotation of full dignity and inclusion and all the other benefits of the word *marriage* are why equality cannot be provided through "another word." Whether the other term used is *civil unions, domestic partnership,* or even *gay marriage,* they are inherently and intentionally separate and unequal. As civil rights leaders such as John Lewis, the last surviving speaker from the great 1963 March on Washington and a hero for all Americans, remind us in declaring their support for full marriage equality, the United States has been down that path before—in the form of separate sections on the bus, separate water fountains, and separate lines at the clerk's office, even separate rules on marriage for the races. We don't need to go there again.

After examining how the civil-union legislation compared with the Jim Crow laws and with the segregation of men and women in education, legal expert Barbara J. Cox similarly concluded:

> The heterosexism inherent in restricting same-sex couples to civil unions is reminiscent of the racism that relegated African-Americans to separate railroad cars and separate schools and of the sexism that relegated women to separate schools. Our society's experiences with "separate but equal" have repeatedly shown that separation can never result in equality because the separation is based on a belief of distance necessary to be maintained between those in the privileged position and those placed in the inferior position.[12]

During the climactic challenges against America's longest and most invidious system of discrimination, Martin Luther King Jr. protested those who urged delay or settling for less than full dignity or equality. King addressed not the bigots and real opponents of equality, but rather those who professed fairness and support for civil rights, the "moderates [who] counted themselves as friends of the civil rights movement . . . [who] had come some distance in step with the thundering drums [of equality] but at the point of [full] application . . . wanted the bugle to sound a retreat." [13]

King lamented the liberals, the moderates, the friends, and, especially, the clergy, who called for "compromise." [14] In stark language he declared:

> What is implied here is the amazing assumption that society has a right to bargain with the Negro for the freedom which inherently belongs to him. Some of the most vocal liberals believe they have a valid basis for demanding that, in order to gain certain rights, the Negro ought to pay for them out of the funds of patience and passivity . . . to accept half a loaf and to pay for that half by waiting willingly for the other half to be distributed in crumbs over a hard and protracted winter of injustice. [15]

Likewise today, when well-meaning allies and politicians in the middle proffer the suggestion that gay Americans will accomplish more by "compromising" or settling for the purportedly more palatable civil unions, all-but-marriage, gay marriage, or piecemeal partnership protections, it's important to remember that you don't get even half a loaf by asking for half a loaf. Americans have learned to ask for, and indeed demand, the whole loaf we all deserve.

This has proven true time and time again, for the states where families have fought the hardest for and, as a result, come the closest to marriage equality are the states that so far offer the most protections for gay and lesbian couples. In Hawaii, for example, the Reciprocal Beneficiaries Law, passed in 1997, was a direct result of the freedom-to-marry campaign there, as discussed in chapter 2. Although full marriage equality in Hawaii was blocked, at least for now, by a massive attack campaign that amended the constitution to prevent the courts from ruling fairly, gay people (and other non-marital families) in Hawaii wound up with the Reciprocal Bene-ficiaries Law, which provides some limited but significant state government rights for unmarried couples. Half a loaf, but first, gay people had to ask and fight for the whole.

Californians got at least half a loaf when they rebelled after being denied a full one. In 2000, opponents of equality pushed a ballot initiative, dubbed Prop. 22, that said California would discriminate against same-sex couples married out of state. Also known as the Knight Initiative, after its sponsor, state Senator William J. "Pete" Knight, the anti-gay proposition passed but nevertheless ratcheted up a statewide conversation that led to a rise in the poll numbers favoring marriage equality. The very next year, in 2001, and again in 2003, the state legislature passed—and the governor signed—two partnership laws. The most recent, the Domestic Partner Rights and Responsibilities Act of 2003, provides gay and lesbian Califor-nians an all-but-marriage option similar to Vermont's civil-union law, but still short of marriage itself in both the intangible impor-tance of equality and tangible protections such as tax-treatment rules for families. And, again, gay couples weren't the only benefi-ciaries of this discussion and partial victory. The same domestic partnership law gives unmarried different-sex couples over age sixty-two the option to choose partnership and secure family pro-tections as well.

Even in Vermont, the civil-union victory did not come by asking for something less than marriage. No, Stan and Peter, Nina and Stacy, and Lois and Holly first had to sue the state for the right to marry. And when the state argued in court that the benefits of mar-riage could be given without the status itself, which could be re-served for only a man and a woman, the couples stood their ground without waving the white flag of "another word." Beth Robinson, one of their attorneys, fired back at the state, comparing its argument to that in favor of interracial-marriage bans fifty years earlier. "The notion of a black and white person marrying was as anathema to many people's notions of marriage as a man marrying a man and a woman marrying a woman," Beth told the court. "The status of marriage is of and in itself a value and a benefit. The state of Vermont cannot have a separate but equal provision here." [16]

The Reverend Al Sharpton puts it even more succinctly, "Marriage—not civil union." Forcing gay couples to settle for civil unions is "like saying we'll give blacks or Latinos the rights to shack up but not marry." [17]

The progress continues. As Lambda Legal's court case moved forward in New Jersey, challenging the different-sex restriction on marriage, the state legislature in January 2004 voted to acknowledge the state's same-sex couples and provide them with some limited but important legal protections that make a real difference to families. Some of the provisions end discrimination in the inheritance-tax exemption, hospital-visitation and medical decision-making rights, and the state income-tax deduction for dependents. Far short of marriage itself, the step toward equality would not have occurred without the push for the freedom to marry.

King's bread analogy proved true in Massachusetts, too, where the state's Supreme Judicial Court made the most conclusive rulings yet in favor of marriage equality. In November 2003, the justices ruled that the state's constitution commands equality for all its citizens and that it therefore requires an end to the exclusion of committed gay couples from marriage. The high court's thoughtful ruling in *Goodridge v. Department of Public Health* stressed the important *intangible* protections and benefits that marriage brings to couples and their children, described the "scarring hardship" caused by the denial of marriage equality, and found that government has no good reason for denying civil marriage licenses and full equality to same-sex couples.[18]

As you can see in the following excerpts from the powerfully reasoned and very readable *Goodridge* opinion, the justices weren't talking about "compromising" equality or using another word:

◆ We construe civil marriage to mean the voluntary union of two persons as spouses, to the exclusion of all others. This reformulation redresses the plaintiff's constitutional injury and furthers the aim of marriage to promote stable, exclusive relationships.

◆ The liberty interest in choosing whether and whom to marry would be hollow if the Commonwealth could, without sufficient justification, foreclose an individual from freely choosing the person with whom to share an exclusive commitment in the unique institution of civil marriage.

◆ Each plaintiff attests a desire to marry his or her partner in order to affirm publicly their commitment to each other and to secure the legal protections and benefits afforded to married couples and their children.

◆ The benefits accessible only by way of marriage license are enormous, touching nearly every aspect of life and death.

◆ Barred access to the protections, benefits, and obligations of civil marriage, a person who enters into an intimate, exclusive union with another of the same sex is arbitrarily deprived of membership in one of our community's most rewarding and cherished institutions.

◆ [Anything but full marriage equality would] confer an official stamp of approval on the destructive stereotype that same-sex relationships are inherently unstable and inferior to opposite-sex relationships and are not worthy of respect.[19]

Indeed, counting up the words in the court's historic opinion shows the following mentions of key terms:

Marriage: 189	Wife: 4
Marry: 36	Spouse: 19
Married: 23	Children: 42
Equality: 13	Family: 19
Equal: 23	Civil union: 0
Husband: 6	

Despite the power and clarity of the *Goodridge* decision, the Massachusetts Legislature again balked at ending marriage discrimination outright. The state Senate filed a request for an advisory opinion, asking the court if a proposed civil-union law would meet the constitutional mandate set forth in *Goodridge*. In February 2004, the justices reiterated that the constitution commands equality, and equal means equal.

"Because the proposed law by its express terms forbids same-sex couples entry into civil marriage, it continues to relegate same-sex couples to a different status," the justices wrote.

The holding in *Goodridge,* by which we are bound, is that group classifications based on unsupportable distinctions, such as that embodied in the proposed bill, are invalid under the Massachusetts Constitution. . . . For no rational reason the marriage laws of the Commonwealth discriminated against a defined class; no amount of tinkering with language will eradicate that stain. The [civil-union] bill would have the effect of maintaining and fostering a stigma of exclusion that the Constitution prohibits. It would deny to same-sex "spouses" only a status that is specially recognized in society and has significant social and other advantages. The Massachusetts Constitution, as was explained in the

Goodridge opinion, does not permit such invidious discrimination, no matter how well intentioned.[20]

The justices summed up the issue and the decision in memorable words: "The history of our nation has demonstrated that separate is seldom, if ever, equal."[21]

As you'll recall, Massachusetts Governor Mitt Romney, a Republican and Mormon, was opposed to both marriage equality and civil unions prior to the high court ruling. When he was campaigning for the governor's office, Romney said, "Call me old fashioned but I don't support gay marriage nor do I support civil union. . . . If a civil union is a Vermont-style civil union, with all of the associated benefits with marriage, then it's the same thing [as marriage] for me for all intents and purposes, and I draw the line there."[22]

Yet after the unequivocal opinion from the Massachusetts court requiring an end to the exclusion of same-sex couples from marriage, Romney declared that in his effort to block full equality by pushing a constitutional amendment, he could support a civil-union outcome. "I believe that a civil union type provision would be sufficient," he said the day after the court ruling. "I believe their decision indicates that a provision which provided benefits, obligation, rights, and responsibilities, which are consistent with marriage but perhaps could be called by a different name, would be in conformity with their decision."[23]

Syndicated columnist Ellen Goodman recently described how the marriage discussion has shifted the center from dismissiveness and opposition toward equality:

> What strikes me in all the fury is how the demilitarized zone has grown. And how, in the culture wars, the middle ground has irrevocably shifted.

Was it just a decade ago when domestic partnerships were considered so radical they were restricted to a few liberal hamlets? In 2000, when the Vermont Legislature approved civil unions, people in the Green Mountain State predicted the sky would fall, the milk would curdle and the maple sap would stop running.

Now civil union has become the moderate position. The argument over the rights of gay partners to marital benefits is nearly ceded. The debate is now about names. . . .

Remember when gay activists were told that this "extremism" would produce a backlash? Instead, it's produced astonishing momentum. Marriage in everything but name has become a new norm.[24]

Congressman Barney Frank notes, correctly, that anti-gay opponents seem to favor civil union only when marriage equality becomes imminent. Only when same-sex couples come within reach of securing the full freedom to marry do our opponents moderate their resistance to any other measure of protection, large or small, for these families. Whenever we ask for, or seem to be settling for, less—or using "another word"—the opposition kicks in anew and seeks to block any recognition of gay families, no matter what the protections or recognition are called. As Beth Robinson related from the Vermont experience, "I never felt like civil unions was a victory. [T]here was a flaw in the political calculation behind civil unions [i.e., that it would be a 'compromise' that eased opposition]. The hell we went through was not any less because it was civil union and not marriage."[25]

Many believe in their hearts that full marriage equality is the right answer and inevitable but still would prefer to dodge the question today by offering support instead for the barely existing option of civil union. Nevertheless, Frank and others (like me) are skeptical of the depth of support for civil union, partnership, or "anything but marriage" that we increasingly hear professed by some politicians and even our opponents in right-wing groups. And sure enough, as the debate in Massachusetts progressed, Governor Romney was exposed as working against civil unions as well as trying to delay and prevent the inevitable nondiscriminatory issuance of marriage licenses required under the state constitution.

Time and again, we have seen that many of those who fight most feverishly against gay people's right to marry also oppose any attempt to extend *any* rights to gay and lesbian couples. For example, California state Senator Pete Knight, the sponsor of that 2000 anti-marriage ballot initiative in that state, asserted during the campaign that the measure would not affect partnership laws, but was "only" about denying recognition to out-of-state marriages of same-sex couples. But once the measure passed, Senator Knight and the others who pushed Proposition 22 campaigned against other family protections for gay people, and have gone to court trying to overturn the broad partnership law passed by the California Legislature and signed into law by the governor in 2003.

And, by the way, Senator Knight's son, David, was among those gay people who got married in San Francisco in 2004. A former Air Force fighter pilot who served in the Gulf War, David Knight, forty-two, and his partner, Joseph Lazzaro, thirty-nine, had been together for more than ten years when they wed at city hall on March 11 in the presence of friends, but no other family members.[26]

There is a question we might want to ask the current converts giving lip service to support for civil unions. Now that they've acknowledged that gay families are worthy of the responsibility, the protections, the security, and the clarity that come with marriage, and now that they've said gay and lesbian families deserve everything that comes with marriage but the word *marriage* itself, just what is it they want to withhold?

If you think about it, the one thing withheld by using a word other than *marriage* is the one thing that, in a free and democratic society, government should not and must not withhold: full equality.

Opponents like to assert that marriage is "defined as between a man and a woman." But, in fact, marriage is not defined by who is excluded from it. The couples seeking the freedom to marry are not asking to change the *definition* of marriage, its responsibilities, or its legal consequences. Rather, they seek to remove a government restriction on the choice of *whom* they can marry with the *same* commitment and legal meaning, just as America has changed other restrictions in the past.

Why should we have two lines at the clerk's office, two sets of rules, two separate and unequal solutions? Why should we say to some kids and couples, "Your families have to come in through the back door?"

Or simply put, why do we need another word?

CHAPTER EIGHT

WILL MARRIAGES IN
ONE STATE BE HONORED
IN OTHERS?

If there is one thing that the people are entitled to expect from their lawmakers, it is rule of law that will enable individuals to tell whether they are married and, if so, to whom.

U.S. Supreme Court Justice Robert Jackson (1948)[1]

Because they're neighbors, they're able to see past the stereotypes and see us as a family and know that we need these rights as a family.

Tony Butterfield, married father of twins, on how his
Salt Lake City, Utah, neighbors responded when he and
his partner got married in San Francisco (2004)[2]

I think it's safe to assume that all of us know couples who got married outside not just their home, but their home state. It's a good bet that many of you reading this book had an out-of-state wedding.

Maybe you wanted to get hitched in Las Vegas, like Paul Newman and Joanne Woodward did in 1958, like Elvis and Priscilla Presley did in 1967, or like Britney Spears and Jason Alexander did (momentarily) in 2004. Perhaps you wanted a romantic ceremony on a beach in Hawaii, like Michelle Pfeiffer and David E. Kelley did in 1993, like Bill and Melinda Gates did in 1994, or like Nicholas Cage and Lisa Marie Presley did in 2002. Or, more likely, maybe you held your wedding away from home because doing so allowed you to get married in the city where your spouse grew up, in the town where you both went to college, or in a location where the greatest number of your friends and family could attend.

Regardless of your reasons for getting married away from home, I doubt that you ever took a break in all your wedding planning—setting the date, choosing the rings, picking the perfect gown, arranging the caterer, and the countless other tasks leading up to the big day—and hired a lawyer to ensure that your marriage would be honored when you returned home from the honeymoon.

Of course you didn't. Even if it had occurred to you to wonder whether your home state would consider your marriage valid even though it was performed somewhere else, with all the other affairs you had to deal with in planning your wedding you would have immediately rejected any such worry as ridiculous. Marriages solemnized in Alaska are recognized in Arizona, just as marriages performed in Oregon are given legal respect in Ohio and Oklahoma. You assumed, as most Americans take for granted, that your marital status would be portable state to state and even country to country. Common sense.

We Americans don't think of marriage certificates as being like tickets that need to be validated before leaving the parking lot at the shopping mall, or like passports we have to get stamped when we cross an international border. Once a couple is married, they're married, and they live their lives as what they are—a legally married couple—regardless of where they held their wedding and regardless of where they live or travel.

Newly married gay and lesbian couples, too, have enough concerns that come with everyday life without having to worry if their marriage—regardless of whether it was celebrated in Canada, Massachusetts, San Francisco, or Portland, Oregon—will be honored when they return home. And just as non-gay newlyweds don't need a marriage visa when returning home from getting married out of state, gay and lesbian newlyweds generally won't go fishing for official "recognition" of their marriage when they come home from their weddings.

After finding places to put their wedding gifts (and probably before they have a chance to write thank-you notes), gay and lesbian newlyweds will get back to the responsibilities of taking care of their homes, working at their jobs, and raising their families. Except for the rings and the wedding announcements in the newspaper, chances are that the rest of us won't be able to tell the difference between these couples and the other same-sex couples we've always seen in our communities. That is, of course, until they identify themselves as married, as people do . . . whether in casual conversation or when filling out a job application, buying a new home, registering their kids for school, checking in at the doctor's office, or filing their tax forms.

That's when the true test—or the metaphorical stamp on the passport, if you will—comes. And that test will have little to do with the way these newly married gay and lesbian couples present themselves, but everything to do with the way the rest of us respond when they do.

So let me ask you, how do you think you would conduct yourself if you came in contact with some of the couples you've already met in this book?

What will you mortgage brokers out there say to Maureen Kilian and Cindy Meneghin, the couple from Butler, New Jersey, who have been together for more than thirty years, when they apply for a mortgage and, in the process, identify themselves as a married couple?

How about you college administrators out there? What will you say to young Annie Goodridge, the daughter of Massachusetts plaintiffs Julie and Hillary Goodridge, when she enrolls as a student at your university and identifies her mothers as married on her financial-aid forms?

And what about all of you retirement-home managers? How would you treat Del Martin and Phyllis Lyon, the couple of fifty-one years who on February 12, 2004, became the first same-sex couple to get married in San Francisco, should they inquire about moving into your assisted-living community and want to live together in the married quarters?

Many Americans already think gay couples can get married, or assume that the long-term couple they've seen at the PTA or shoveling snow out of the driveway are already married. If you're one of those Americans, you probably won't bat an eye.

If you're like many people when they encounter something they're unaccustomed to, you might be a bit surprised when a gay or lesbian couple first identifies themselves to you as married. But after a moment, perhaps, whether you're a mortgage broker, a college administrator, a retirement-home manager, or simply Joe or Jo Citizen meeting the couple on the street, you'll probably acknowledge the couple for what they are—a legally married couple—even if for no other reason than that it's a lot easier to do that than to confront the couple and try to prove that they aren't, in fact, married. And the next time you meet a married same-sex couple you'll be less surprised.

But what about those mortgage brokers, college administrators, and retirement-home managers who have a moral or political objection to gay people? How do you think they'll respond to Maureen Kilian and Cindy Meneghin, to Annie or Julie and Hillary Goodridge, or to Del Martin and Phyllis Lyon? Chances are that many of them, too, will acknowledge (even if they may or may not fully accept) these couples for what they are and for the family structures that the state has said they have. Most Americans believe in "live and let live," realizing that accepting differences is part of life in a free country. And, of course, others more disapproving will nevertheless treat the marriages with begrudging equality, because, again, it will be considerably less comfortable to do anything but that. Most people are not going to take it upon themselves to deny someone else's marriage face-to-face.

In fact, except in cases where they're constrained by discriminatory law—or in the inevitable incidents involving die-hard anti-gay bigots—most Americans are going to want to be fair, decent, and neighborly. Most Americans will be inclined to honor the actual marriage of the real people standing before them. It's much easier to be against something in the hypothetical than it is to look a family in the face and take it upon yourself to say "No."

* * *

Now, at this point, I imagine some of you are saying to yourself, "But gay and lesbian couples aren't yet allowed to get married in my state. Doesn't that mean their marriages won't be honored here?"

Before I directly answer that question, let me point out a couple of other kinds of marriages that might not be allowed in your state but are nevertheless honored in every state. Currently, only twenty-six states allow first cousins to marry each other. But do those married first cousins worry about whether their marriage is "recognized" if they move to or visit one of the twenty-four states that don't allow first-cousin marriages? Nope. Their marriages are considered marriages regardless of where they live or travel; no one today thinks the reasons to discriminate against their marriages outweigh the logic of respecting their families and marital status.

Or another example: States differ in how old (or young) people can be before they marry, and some states require parental approval before couples under a certain age (at ages other states think inappropriate for marriage) can marry each other. Nevertheless, young couples who get married in states without such a law are not required to get permission slips signed before crossing the border into a parental-approval state, or a state with a higher age limit. They are as married in Texas as they are in Tennessee, regardless of any discrepancies in those states' laws on who can marry whom.

This cooperation between states is called "comity," and it didn't come about because of some sweeping statement the president made regarding the sanctity of first-cousin marriages. Nor is it necessarily a reflection of any constitutional compulsion that commands states to honor out-of-state lawful marriages, although there are constitutional principles and provisions that apply, including equal protection; federalism, guarantees of national citizenship and unity, and the right to mobility; and the fundamental right to marry itself. Instead, this comity is a result of states realizing—on a voluntary, rational, thinking-it-out basis—that there are simply better and more valuable reasons for honoring people's marriages than there are for destabilizing them.

After all, imagine if married couples had to worry if their right to inherit from each other remained valid, or if their right to make medical decisions for each other (or their children) would be respected, or if their family health plan was in force—merely because they chose to move to or visit another state. Imagine the difficulty for a bank in their home state that had loaned money based on a spousal guarantee that was enforceable in that state, only to learn it would not be enforced by a sister state. How could a company maintain coherent personnel policies if its offices were required by conflicting state laws to treat the same employees as simultaneously married and unmarried depending on the office in which they worked? How could a couple be sure their expectations for Social Security or veterans' benefits, child or spousal support, property and insurance rates, or the myriad other ways marriage affects one's life economically and legally would be honored?

It's common sense: We don't want couples to have to worry if they're married or not depending on where they are. We don't want kids to worry whether their parents are still married when they go on vacation. And we don't want banks and businesses to wonder whether their contracts are still good if their customers have crossed a border.

For more than two hundred years of American history, states have taken these sound policy reasons for honoring marriages and made them into a general principle of law: A marriage that is valid where celebrated will generally be honored elsewhere, even in a place that would not itself have performed the marriage.

Even in the era of interracial marriage bans, when many states made it illegal to marry someone of the "wrong" race, they still almost always honored those marriages performed elsewhere.[3] Even states (like the Lovings' Virginia) that made it a *crime* to perform such marriages or to engage in such a marriage in their state—the harshest form of legal disapproval—generally understood that when married couples were traveling from one state to another or were moving from one part of the country to another, their marriages should be left intact.

As of yet, no state has gone so far as to make it a crime for gay people to marry, nor has any explained exactly how it benefits the state and others, let alone the couple and their kids, more to sunder the marriages than to acknowledge them.

And, as we've discussed before, there was a time in our country when the same kinds of groups speaking out so adamantly against gay people's freedom to marry were thumping the table and saying it was against God's law and the very "definition" of marriage to allow couples to get out of failed marriages. As a result, there used to be a great disparity among states regarding divorce. Some permitted it, and others didn't. Many people had to leave their home states in order to end their failed marriages, and when they returned home, in some cases the states refused to recognize their divorce. Preachy states held these married people to be "locked in for life," regardless of their wishes and circumstances, or any divorce granted out of state.

Naturally, these discrepancies led to a patchwork, which led to litigation, and several of the court cases went all the way to the U.S. Supreme Court. In a series of decisions over time, the justices eventually concluded that it is intolerable to have a country where people don't know from day to day or state to state whether or not they are married. As Justice Robert Jackson wrote in 1948 in his dissent in one of the earlier cases, *Estin v. Estin,* "If there is one thing that the people are entitled to expect from their lawmakers, it is rule of law that will enable individuals to tell whether they are married and, if so, to whom." The lawmakers eventually followed.

Gay and lesbian married couples are entitled to expect the same thing from their lawmakers. Unless America creates a "gay exception" to common sense, legal precedents, and the tradition and actual practice of the states throughout history, these legally married couples, too, should get nothing less than equal treatment, meaning full marital obligations, recognition, and portability.

But, in fact, right-wing groups *are* now pressuring politicians to create just such a gay exception, seeking to stampede lawmakers into carving gay people and gay couples' marriages out of the commonsense principles and practice by which states and our country have always resolved these legal differences over time.

As countries such as Canada, states such as Massachusetts, and cities such as San Francisco continue to open the doors of marriage to committed same-sex couples, we can look to these historical examples to see a pattern in the way our country deals with such differences in marriage laws.

First there is a period when some states move in the direction of equality and inclusion, while other states dig in their heels or pile on resistance and discrimination. By its very nature, this patchwork period generates a lot of discussion—in public forums, in the media, and at the kitchen table—about the impact on families. More and more people begin to hear stories, listen to the arguments made by opponents, consider how they'd want to be treated if they were in the same boat, and figure out where they stand with regard to the nation's treatment of a group of fellow citizens they gradually come to understand better.

Generally, even during these patchwork periods, states have honored the marriages from other states—again, for the sound policy reasons discussed earlier. In fact, if you read all of the court cases in which these questions have ever been dealt with (and experts like Professor Barb Cox, colleagues at Lambda Legal, my team, and myself have indeed done just that), in virtually every one, when push came to shove, and no matter what the states said they were going to do hypothetically, ultimately they almost always honored the marriages before them.

So, now to answer the question asked earlier: How will gay couples' marriages be treated in states that do not allow them to marry?

For a period of time, there will be a patchwork. Some states will honor the marriages between gay or lesbian couples because it makes no sense to sunder those bonds and it is wrong to treat one group of Americans' marriages differently from all others. Equally predictably, for a time other states—the resisters—will look for ways to reinforce their existing anti-gay laws and their denial of any protections or support to gay families. The anti-gay campaign formally under way, as we discussed in chapter 2, since 1996 will continue its drive to make America a "house divided" to suit these groups' own "culture war" agenda and political purposes. Employers, businesses, officials, and courts will grapple with the new reality of married couples standing before them, and some will find themselves constrained by discriminatory laws to deny these families, while others will find a way to do the right thing. The federal government, because of the so-called "Defense of Marriage Act" discussed earlier, will, for a time, discriminate: second-class marriages for second-class citizens.

There will be litigation, though for every case in court there will be thousands of other day-to-day moments in which gay married couples and their kids encounter a mix of respect, discrimination, and uncertainty from the institutions and neighbors they deal with. Some of the discrimination and refusal to honor the marriages will be ugly, painful, and injurious; people will lose their jobs, face deportation, be denied health coverage, and more. To guide same-sex couples in making decisions about how to deal with this discrimination, all of the leading lesbian and gay legal groups—Lambda Legal, GLAD, the National Center for Lesbian Rights, and the

ACLU Lesbian/Gay Rights Project—have prepared advisories and Q&As, which can be found on Freedom to Marry's Web site, www.freedomtomarry.org.[4]

But faced with real, live, legally married couples and their kids, more and more people, even recalcitrant states, and eventually the federal government will over time generally tend toward honoring these marriages. And the law will change, as the reality that ending marriage discrimination helps families and harms no one continues to sink in, and as more and more Americans in more and more states are touched, once again, by the better angels of their nature.

Such has already been the experience of P. J. Sedillo and Tony Ross of Albuquerque, New Mexico, who were married in Canada in October 2003. Before the couple got married, P. J.'s employer, the Albuquerque school district, refused his request to provide health coverage to Tony. But after he and Tony tied the knot, P. J. presented the employment benefits manager at the school district with a copy of their marriage certificate and, three weeks later, he received a letter from his insurance company indicating that Tony was now eligible for insurance coverage—although as a domestic partner.[5]

As more couples like P. J. and Tony introduce themselves to their neighbors and to their employers as the legally married couples that they are, eventually it will no longer be a question of debate that gay and lesbian families exist and that they, too, need the protections and responsibilities that marriage can provide.

The pattern of American history is that after a period of time, debate, and patchwork, the nation moves toward resolution and equality.

In the case of divorce, the discrepancies were resolved because the sheer mess of some states saying a couple isn't married and other states saying "yes, they are" became intolerable. In the long struggle over racial discrimination in marriage, there were a handful of cases in which courts found states constitutionally required to honor the disfavored interracial marriages, but the overwhelming bulk of the 200-plus years' worth of court cases dealing with the issue were decided on common sense and comity. Ultimately, as we have seen, the underlying discrimination itself was struck down by the U.S. Supreme Court—fully nineteen years after the first state court had done so.

Never before in all this country's history of civil rights battles over marriage, never before amid all the discrepancies from state to state over who can marry whom and whether to permit divorce, never before has a president proposed to rewrite the federal Constitution so as to end the discussion or take the decision away from the states, lawmakers, and the courts. Bad as it is to force families to deal with a mix of respect, discrimination, and uncertainty such as inheres in a patchwork period, it would be worse to deprive states, our nation, and future generations of the chance to make the decisions about marriage equality.

Americans are starting to ask themselves whether the law should continue to have a gay exception to the way we treat families, commitment, and people who cross state borders in this, our country. Or should gay couples willing to play by the rules get the same rules to play by?

America is one country, not fifty separate kingdoms. If you're married, you're married. Common sense.

CHAPTER NINE

IS MARRIAGE
EQUALITY A QUESTION
OF CIVIL RIGHTS?

My husband, Martin Luther King Jr., understood that all forms of discrimination and persecution were unjust and unacceptable for a great democracy. He believed that none of us could be free until all of us were free, that a person of conscience had no alternative but to defend the human rights of all people. . . . The civil rights movement that I believe in thrives on unity and inclusion, not division and exclusion. All of us who oppose discrimination and support equal rights should stand together to resist every attempt to restrict civil rights in this country.

Coretta Scott King, an early endorser of the
Marriage Resolution in support of gay people's
freedom to marry (2000) [1]

If I had married when I was supposed to, I would have lost my name, my legal residence, my credit rating, my ability to get a loan or start a business without my husband's

permission—most of my civil rights. . . . I have always sup-
ported same-sex marriage, but in retrospect, I think I didn't
fully understand the desire to say not just "we are living
together," or "we love each other," but "we are responsible for
each other." Now I do. I pledge myself to work that much
harder to make marriage a democratic institution open to
everyone, whether or not there are children, a chosen part-
nership.

Gloria Steinem, another Marriage Resolution
signatory (2001)[2]

The United States has always prided itself on its commitment to liberty and equality. And while our country has sometimes fallen short in its fulfillment of these human rights, we Americans have almost always rallied in large numbers around important civil rights campaigns—from the abolitionist and suffrage movements of the nineteenth century to the racial equality and women's movements of the twentieth century. Now, with Massachusetts becoming the first state to end sex discrimination in marriage, and with a growing number of the nation's mayors issuing marriage licenses to gay couples rather than bowing to political pressure, it's clear that one of the first important civil rights campaigns of the twenty-first century is well under way: the movement for gay people's freedom to marry.

It's altogether fitting and proper, as well as inevitable, that this civil rights campaign prompts comparisons to those battles that came before it. When San Francisco's Mayor Gavin Newsom started issuing marriage licenses to same-sex couples in February 2004, he said, "Rosa Parks didn't wait for the courts to tell her it was all right to ride in the front of the bus." [3] A couple of weeks later, when Mayor Jason West of New Paltz, New York, solemnized Michele Yasson's marriage to Lauren Warren (along with the marriages of twenty-four other same-sex couples), Yasson told a reporter, "We're here to fight for our civil rights so we don't have to sit in the back of the bus anymore." [4] And after Diane Linn, the county chair in Multnomah County, Oregon, directed officials in March 2004 to issue marriage licenses to gay and lesbian couples, newly married couple Karen Lane and Janine Zeller said they were "on the verge of the largest civil rights movement since Martin Luther King."[5]

Similarly, when the Massachusetts state legislature convened a constitutional convention in early 2004 to discuss options to block the high court ruling mandating marriage equality, several lawmakers made strong—and passionate—parallels between the freedom-to-marry and other civil rights campaigns. State Senator Diane Wilkerson was in tears as she told fellow legislators her memories of growing up black in Arkansas, where her mother was not allowed to give birth in the public hospital. "I know the pain of being less than equal and I cannot and will not impose that status on anyone else," she said. "I was but one generation removed from an existence in slavery. I could not in good conscience ever vote to send anyone to that place from which my family fled."[6]

House Assistant Majority Leader Lida Harkins recalled taking part in a civil rights march in the 1960s. "As Lincoln said, this nation was conceived in liberty and dedicated to the proposition that all men are created equal," she told her fellow legislators. "I have marched with Martin Luther King to this common in Boston to support civil rights. Today I will cast another civil rights vote in defense of our constitution."[7]

State Representative Alice Wolf, meanwhile, another supporter of marriage equality, talked about growing up in Austria during the Holocaust. "My parents could not take me to the local playground because we had to wear a yellow star because we were a Jewish family. Others wore other colored stars. There were gays and lesbians, Catholics, and gypsies," she said, adding that she was sent to live in a small town where her parents felt she would be out of danger. "The rest, I guess you could say, is history because we were able to come to this wonderful country, and I can stand here and explain this to you."[8]

Mind you, it is not only this latest confluence of events around the fight for marriage equality that has triggered these comparisons. The true theory of civil rights protection is that because each person is equally special, it is especially important that each person be equally protected. Thus, civil rights veterans have long embraced equal rights for gay men and lesbians and considered the battle for our equality a part of this nation's larger civil rights struggle. Indeed, aside from concerns for principle and solidarity, many gay Americans are black *and* gay, female *and* Asian, or Jewish *and* lesbian. Bayard Rustin, one of the chief architects of the racial equality movement in this country, the lead planner of the epochal 1963 March on Washington, and a close friend of Martin Luther King Jr., was himself a gay man, as King and other colleagues knew.

King's widow, Coretta Scott King, was an early endorser of the Marriage Resolution in support of gay people's freedom to marry. Speaking at a Lambda Legal event in 1998, she repeated her strong commitment to inclusion and belief that gay rights are part of civil rights: "I still hear people say that I should not be talking about the rights of lesbian and gay people and I should stick to the issue of racial justice . . . But I hasten to remind them that Martin Luther King Jr. said, 'Injustice anywhere is a threat to justice everywhere.' "[9]

On the fortieth anniversary of the March on Washington, U.S. Representative John Lewis, who is the last surviving speaker from the March and a strong supporter of gay people's equal freedom to marry, declared,

> We must recapture the spirit that we had forty years ago. As a
> nation and as a people, we must make this spirit part of our
> thoughts—our action in our lives. If we do this, we can make

Dr. Martin Luther King's dream come true. We can build what he called a beloved community—a truly interracial democracy, a community at peace with itself. All of us, black and white, Hispanic, Asian-American, and Native American, gays and straights, Protestant, Catholic, Jews, and Muslims, must pull together for the common good. This is our mission.[10]

However, today some opponents of marriage equality strain mightily to obscure the pro-gay positions of these notable civil rights leaders. They wish to persuade Americans that gay people's quest for equality is something wholly different, something entirely separate from the other civil rights struggles that have enriched our nation's history.

"Skin color or ethnicity involves no moral choices . . . but how you conduct yourself sexually does," said Robert Knight, whom I debated on *Nightline* when he was at the Family Research Council and is now housed at another far-right group, the Concerned Women for America (a group, like most of our opponents, not notably concerned about racial equality in any other context). Gay people and non-gay allies "are trying to hijack the moral capital of the black civil rights movement and use it to force society to affirm their behavior, regardless of other people's moral beliefs about it."[11]

Debra J. Saunders, a columnist for the *San Francisco Chronicle*, took issue with Mayor Newsom's comparison between Rosa Parks and the gay couples who were flocking to San Francisco to get married. "How can anyone compare Parks' experience with that of San Francisco's same-sex newlyweds?" she wrote. "They don't face arrest. They won't be jailed. They won't be fined. City Hall is sponsoring the ceremonies. Why, the City Hall café sold splits of Champagne so there would be bubbly at last weekend's wedding. Civil disobedience? Hardly."[12]

Right-wing groups pursuing their anti-gay and anti-separation-of-church-and-state agendas have taken to showcasing those members of the black clergy who say they are offended by the civil rights parallels drawn by NAACP chair Julian Bond, Mrs. King, and others. These clergy characterize gay identity as but a "lifestyle" and thus see no parallel to discrimination based on a trait, such as race, that is not "chosen." "As an African-American, I find it highly offensive to associate homosexuality with civil rights," says the Reverend Steven Craft, a retired pastor from New Brunswick, New Jersey. "People have been trying to run on that civil rights banner and to use this whole idea of homosexual marriage to say it's the next wave of the movement. But race and sexuality have nothing to do with each other." [13]

The vocal presence of some African-American clergy brought by right-wing groups to testify in favor of a proposed anti-gay amendment to the Massachusetts Constitution earned a strong rebuke from an African-American state representative. As the *Boston Globe* reported:

> Representative Byron Rushing said the Legislature was in danger of making the state constitution look like an object that belonged "in the days before the Civil War." Rushing, who is black, took black religious leaders to task for coming out against gay marriage, which he said is an issue of basic civil rights. "I am saying to that small group of leaders, shame on you," said Rushing, a Democrat from Boston's South End. [14]

After a March 2004 speech reaffirming her support for marriage equality and her opposition to constitutional amendments that would discriminate against gay Americans, Coretta Scott King labeled the anti-gay stand taken by some African-American clergy "misinformed."[15] But one clergyman, the Reverend Gregory Daniels, an African-American Baptist minister from Chicago, went so far as to declare, "If the K.K.K. opposed gay marriage, I would ride with them."[16]

Clearly there is something deeper here than a mere disagreement over historical analogies.

Anti-gay groups are aware of the respect most Americans today have for the civil rights movement of the 1950s and '60s. They know how much most Americans cherish the idea of equality, and understand that if they can successfully distinguish gay and lesbian rights—and the freedom-to-marry movement, specifically—from this country's overall commitment to civil rights, they will have cleared one of the tallest hurdles in their campaign to get Americans to oppose marriage equality. After all, if people believe that gay rights are something "other" than the civil rights campaigns so many Americans have historically embraced as being a key to this country's character, it's not too much of a stretch to get those same people to believe that granting gay and lesbian couples the right to marry might actually be bad for this country.

So whom are we to believe? Are gay couples part of a greater human fabric, and are gay people's rights and freedom connected to the rights and freedom of all Americans, as Bishop Desmond Tutu, Coretta Scott King, Congressman John Lewis, and NAACP chair Julian Bond tell us? Or does the human rights movement for gay equality have absolutely nothing to do with the abolitionist, suffrage, racial equality, and women's movements that came before it, as our opponents suggest?

Let me start by saying up front that our country's struggles over racial equality and social justice have been a defining theme of American history since before the United States was born, with racial minorities experiencing extraordinary violence, injustice, and inhumanity. One has only to read the works of historians like David Garrow, who has written extensively on both the racial justice and women's equality movements, or the memoirs of heroes such as John Lewis's *Walking with the Wind* to appreciate the courage it took to stand up against what today is nearly unimaginable intimidation and oppression.[17] African-Americans today still must deal with indignities, cumulative economic disadvantage, and the legacies of lingering exclusion and unfairness, one example of which is how black lesbians and gay men, such as those who formed the National Black Justice Coalition, are often rendered invisible in debates among gays and among blacks, as well as in the national discourse that ignores the overlap in the groups and gay people of color's intersecting identities.[18] As we will discuss below, comparisons are not to be drawn lightly and must be respectful of historical differences, as well as commonalities.

Still, as we've already seen in previous chapters in this book, there are many parallels that can be drawn between the gay rights movement and the civil rights movements that preceded it.[19] That's true even if you limit the comparisons to struggles over marriage.

Marriage, as we have seen, has always been a battleground for larger questions of inclusion, equality, the separation of church and state, and the proper boundary between individual choice and government interference. African-Americans were denied the right to marry altogether as a way of denying their full humanity; in some states, Asian-Americans and members of minority faiths faced marriage discrimination; in the infamous Nuremberg laws aimed at shoving the Jews outside the status of citizen and ultimately person, restricting the freedom to marry had a central place.

And before the obstacles to divorce were removed in the 1940s and 1950s, before married and unmarried couples could decide for themselves whether to use contraception, before legal race discrimination in marriage ended in 1967, and before laws making wives legally inferior to their husbands were taken off the books in the 1970s and 1980s, the opponents of change were making the same predictions they're making today: The institution of marriage and civilization itself will be destroyed if the discrimination ends. Each and every time opponents of equality said the proposed change was "against the definition of marriage" and "against God's will." In his 1996 book, *One More River to Cross: Black & Gay in America,* Keith Boykin, founder of the National Black Justice Coalition, devoted an entire chapter to "The Common Language of Racism and Homophobia," noting that arguments once used to justify segregation and racial oppression now figure in the right wing's anti-gay campaign.[20]

Fortunately, as we also discussed earlier, Americans have always rejected the "sky is falling" argument and instead made marriage a more inclusive and fair commitment of equals.

There are more poetic civil rights parallels as well. It was in Massachusetts, our nation's "Cradle of Liberty," that slavery was first abolished in a court decision, *Jennison v. Caldwell,* in 1783. How fitting that in 2003, it was again in Massachusetts that a court decision, *Goodridge v. Department of Public Health,* became the first to abolish sex discrimination in marriage.

It is poetic and fitting, too, that May 17, 2004, the day the *Goodridge* decision required that state officials begin the nondiscriminatory issuance of marriage licenses to gay and lesbian couples, marked the fiftieth anniversary of the U.S. Supreme Court's momentous decision in *Brown v. Board of Education* condemning "separate and unequal" segregation in the nation's schools.

For years now, marriage equality groups have celebrated February 12 as National Freedom to Marry Day, a date chosen because of Lincoln's birthday and the lead-up to Valentine's Day—signifying the key themes of equality and love. Each year around Freedom to Marry Day, couples and organizations have held events such as clergy prayer breakfasts, town-hall meetings, letter-writing campaigns, and demonstrations at marriage license bureaus to call attention to the denial of the right to marry and to reach out to ask for non-gay support.

In 2004 National Freedom to Marry Day brought new civil rights poetry. It was in California in 1948 that a court first ended race discrimination in marriage (also, as in *Goodridge,* by a vote of four to three). Thanks to the profile in courage shown by San Francisco's Mayor Gavin Newsom, California again led the nation on this latest civil rights frontier, when on February 12, 2004, city officials began issuing marriage licenses without discrimination. America got to see thousands of couples lining up outside San Francisco's magnificent City Hall—some waiting overnight, some in the rain, some bringing their kids and their parents—not to do violence, not to protest, not to take anything away from anyone else, but to get married.

America got to meet Del Martin and Phyllis Lyon, the first same-sex couple to get legally married in San Francisco. Del, eighty-three, and Phyllis, seventy-nine, were already well known to gay people for their lifetime of contributions to the community, including founding America's first national lesbian rights organization, the Daughters of Bilitis, in 1955, the year of the Montgomery bus boycott. Some call them the "matriarchs" of our civil rights movement. Del and Phyllis got married on February 12, and celebrated their fifty-first anniversary together two days later on Valentine's Day. After more than half a century of personal commitment to each other, these women had waited long enough and deserved the legal commitment of marriage without discrimination from the government.

Other non-gay voices spoke up. In an editorial entitled "It's a Question of Rights," *La Opinión,* the nation's largest Spanish language daily paper, said:

> The legal acts of the last few days in the municipality of San Francisco should be respected for correcting an injustice in the law. The institution of matrimony is not endangered by the civil marriages of homosexuals . . . The rights and obligations that everyone should have before the law is a matter for all responsible human beings no matter what their private preference.[21]

The spirit of Rosa Parks, the embodiment of courageous willingness to challenge wrong, indeed inspires many of these couples and many of the non-gay supporters speaking up today for marriage equality—voices that have begun to include young, white, Catholic, non-gay elected officials such as Mayor Newsom as well as the older white, Catholic, non-gay mayor of Chicago, Richard Daley Jr.; other Democrats, such as Congresswoman Nancy Pelosi, the ranking Democrat in the House of Representatives; and Republicans, such as California Governor Arnold Schwarzenegger.

Let us note, however, that the comparison to Rosa Parks is not a perfect fit. This is not just because the violence and exclusion African-Americans confronted in Montgomery, Alabama, in the 1950s were so massive. Although the lives of human rights pioneers such as Phyllis and Del have ample resonance with the example of Rosa Parks, the decisions made by Mayor Newsom and the elected officials and clerks around the country to issue marriage licenses to committed same-sex couples is not, in my view, best understood as civil disobedience, a venerable and valid form of activism. Rather, it is constitutional *obedience*—these officials are following, not flouting the law. By issuing licenses without discrimination, they are doing what the law permits and the Constitution requires. And far from refusing to obey an unjust law, they are submitting the question to the courts, who will decide, as the courts should, whether there is sufficient reason to continue the exclusion of same-sex couples or, rather, whether constitutional guarantees of equality under the law mean that marriage discrimination must end.

As Professor Henry Louis Gates Jr., the chair of Harvard's African and African-American Studies Department, once summed up the question of the comparisons between the civil rights struggles of gay men and lesbians on one hand, and African-Americans on the other: It "isn't that there's simply no comparison; it's that there's no simple comparison."[22]

Every civil rights campaign has its own particularities as well as certain commonalities with others in the greater movement for human rights. The same is true for the prejudices that each group faces. For example, in his essay "Blacklash?" written during the 1993 debate over ending anti-gay discrimination in the military, Gates observes that "anti-black racism charges its object with inferiority, [while] anti-Semitism charges its object with iniquity. The racist believes that blacks are incapable of running anything by themselves. The anti-Semite believes that 13 rabbis . . . rule the world"[23] Differences, yes, but commonalities in the end result—stigma, harm, and exclusion for a disfavored minority—and in the claims and attacks by the opponents of equality.

Although African-Americans' history differs from that of, say, Jews, Latinos, or women, clearly all these groups have experienced prejudice, discrimination, and violence. Notwithstanding critical historical differences, and without trying to establish a hierarchy of which is worse, our country's civil rights laws place the prohibition against sex-based, racial, or religious discrimination into the same provisions. Americans are as equally protected against discrimination based on race and sex as they are against discrimination based on religion.

This is the case even though an individual's religious belief is, of course, a matter of "choice," while sex or race is generally viewed as "beyond one's control."

So why are protections against anti-gay discrimination, or, more broadly, the guarantee of equal rights regardless of sexual orientation, gay or non-gay, treated any differently? One of our opponents' favorite responses to that question is to talk about the difference between what they are now pleased to call "benign characteristics" such as race (though, of course, many of these same people were hardly so benign about race thirty years ago) and "conduct/choice/lifestyle," which is how they characterize sexual orientation.

But that response ignores the fact that as demonstrated by the anti-bias protections available to both African-Americans and Jews, there have long been two paradigms of civil rights protection in this country: one based on race and the other based on religion. And though when we hear the words "civil rights" today we often think of race, in fact the religious paradigm for equal rights is the older, the one that figured most prominently in the Constitution as framed by our nation's founders. While bitterly divided—as our country has been—on the question of race, the framers of the Constitution clearly intended to secure full protections for Americans in religion, protections that thereby apply to matters of conscience, of practices, of association, and of choice.

In the words of James Madison, the greatest danger to liberty is "faction . . . a number of citizens, whether amounting to a majority or a minority of the whole, who are united and actuated by some common impulse of passion, or of interest, adverse to the rights of other citizens, or to the permanent and aggregate interests of the community."[24] Despite this fear of faction, the framers of the Constitution and the Bill of Rights did not sacrifice individual liberty. Instead, they celebrated the freedom of individuals and groups—as well as the resulting diversity, different opinions, practices, and choices that freedom produces. Intrusion on this right of choice, whether by a faction or against a faction, was unacceptable in their eyes.

As Madison explained, "In a free government, the security for civil rights must be the same as that for religious rights. It consists in the one case in the multiplicity of interests, and in the other in the multiplicity of sects. The degree of security in both cases will depend on the number of interests and sects."[25]

What Madison's words show us is that in American democratic thought we find *instrumental* value in diversity—based on the liberty of choice—as well as *intrinsic* value in the human liberty of exercising one's own right of conscience and deciding how to live life. U.S. Supreme Court Justice Louis D. Brandeis put it this way: "Those who won our independence believed that the final end of the State was to make men free to develop their own faculties. . . . They valued liberty both as an end and as a means. They believed liberty to be the secret of happiness."[26] Religious difference is protected, in part, *because* it is a matter of choice. Protection of choice, and difference—in religion, in opinion, in identity, in expression, and in intimate association—is the true moral vision of our American Constitution. Diversity and choice help keep us all free.

As gay people and as Americans, we want what all human beings deserve: both the right to be different and the right to be equal. We want our freedom to make personal choices in life, to pursue happiness. And as Americans, gay and non-gay, we must proudly make and support these aspirations as our contribution to the human rights progress of history. No American, no human being, should have to give up her or his difference in order to be treated equally under the law.

There is thus a "special" irony that so many of those leading today's "culture war" on gay civil rights and Americans' right to choose garb themselves in sanctimonious trappings. Which group would they have been part of in the equivalent struggles of the past: those seeking protection for their chosen exercise of conscience and practices, or those burning others because of their choice, their conduct, their "lifestyle"? Better that we all should heed the words of yet another founder, Alexander Hamilton: "No man can be sure that he may not be tomorrow the victim of a spirit of injustice, by which he may be a gainer today." [27]

And by the way, when I use the word *choice,* I don't mean to grant any credence to another scripted talking point of anti-gay organizations: that gay and non-gay people "choose" their sexual orientation, that it's a mere "lifestyle." As most of us know by now, even though science cannot fully answer how a predominant attraction to others of the same or different sex is determined, there is enough evidence to show that sexual orientation is not something people choose consciously one day, or can easily change. My non-gay parents have a gay son, me. And few people can point to a day when they woke up and made a choice to be, or not to be, gay.

Nevertheless, this argument is a favorite excuse of those who try to distinguish gay rights from civil rights. "We're not discriminating against you because of who you are, but because of the choices you make and the things that you do," they say, as if that helps.

Here, too, Gates offers a trenchant observation about what he called "the vexed distinction between 'status' and 'behavior.' " He writes, "Most people think of racial identity as a matter of (racial) status, but they respond to it as behavior. Most people think of sexual identity as a matter of (sexual) behavior, but they respond to it as status." [28]

Racists, Gates explains, justify their hatred of African-Americans (a "status") in stereotypes related to violence; to the social pathologies of urban poverty, drugs, and dependency ("behaviors"); and the irresponsibility and inferiority the pathologies project.

Those who are anti-gay, meanwhile, hate gay people as a class, supposedly because of sexual practices ("behaviors"). However, those sexual practices are rarely present in most settings in which most non-gay people encounter gay men and lesbians (for example, in the workplace, or while on military service, or at a wedding). What's more, the particular sex acts may or may not be indulged in by any particular gay person or couple, and most are not confined to lesbians and gay men. When was the last time you heard of a non-gay person denied the right to serve in the military or get married because he might engage in oral sex?

Despite these inconvenient truths, anti-gay hostility justified by reference to "behavior" or "choices" becomes prejudice and discrimination based on gay "status" or identity. In Gates's words, "Disapproval of a sexual practice is transmuted into the demonization of a sexual species." And, in turn, this hostility becomes free-floating and inescapable, regardless of any connection to any gay person's actual conduct, choices, behavior, or "lifestyle," and is used to irrationally deny gay couples even the ability to do the very things that one would think true conservatives or people who profess a religion of love would want them to do: commit to partners, care for others, take on responsibilities, join the community, marry.

So, of racial, religious, and sexual-orientation-based discrimination, which is based on identity and which is based on choices? Which is based on inherent characteristics and which is based on "behavior"?

But perhaps most important, what difference does the taxonomy of oppression or the etiology of prejudice make when it comes to protecting people from the end result: discrimination, hatred, violence, and the loss to society of each person's full potential?

Opponents of equal marriage say equal rights shouldn't be extended on the basis of sexual orientation because gay people, unlike other victims of discrimination, are not really oppressed. Explaining his cosponsorship of a proposed constitutional amendment to ban marriage equality, Massachusetts state Representative Mark J. Carron said, "[Pro-marriage advocates] say it's a civil rights issue. [But] are gay people denied the right to vote? Are they denied employment? Are they denied home ownership?" [29]

Well, putting aside for a moment the ongoing campaign to amend state and federal constitutions so as to mandate gay legal inferiority for all time—a fairly oppressive and historically radical piece of discrimination in and of itself—the answer to the state representative's question is, quite simply, Yes, under existing law in most states and without any federal civil rights law to the contrary, gay people can be denied employment just because of being gay. It is legal in most states to refuse to sell a gay person a home, or rent her an apartment, or serve her in a restaurant—absent civil rights laws to the contrary—and it happens. How can politicians busy pushing additional anti-gay laws not know that and not care?

Gay Americans are also discriminated against while serving their country in the armed forces; denied health coverage and Social Security for their partners and often their kids; impeded in adopting children; denied custody of their biological children; and even beaten and killed in city streets and parks—all because of their sexual orientation.

Vermont state Representative Bill Lippert, an openly gay legislator, put it best. During that state's 2000 debate on marriage and civil unions, he said, "We argue about whether they are civil rights or other rights. But I'll tell you this, they are rights that I don't have right now and most everyone else in this chamber does."[30]

While the history of race discrimination in our country is extensive, brutal, ongoing—and, I believe, unparalleled in its violence, harm, and impact—as Gates points out, "trying to establish a pecking order of oppression is generally a waste of time."[31] In the words of Nadine Smith, an African-American lesbian organizer in the South, "Sometimes this question is phrased in a way that plays into the hands of bigots by asking people to rank oppression[,] asking people 'Who has it worse?' . . . I've experienced racism, sexism and homophobia. And the worst one is whatever one you're dealing with right now."[32]

Moreover, for each group's comparative advantage, we can come up with a disadvantage. For instance, most African-Americans or Asians cannot "pass" or escape crude discrimination as easily as most gay people and some Latinos, Jews, or Baptists (though some African-Americans can pass, while some gay people, Latinos, and others are unmistakable). But on the other hand, most gay men and lesbians are not born into families and networks that share our difference. Rather, we have to make our way on our own, often after years of hostile socialization not only from society, but from the very institutions other minorities usually rely on for self-worth and solidarity, including even our own families. Gay kids often are most afraid of coming out to the very people other minorities count on for support and strength—their own parents and peers. And the ability to "pass" means that many gay people need not partake in gay identity, or help in the fight against discrimination, or even be counted as voters or voices who might move others.[33]

Should the price of equality and inclusion in America be that you have to pass, hide, conform, or abandon what makes you different? Is that the best we have to offer our kids?

What opponents of gay equality ultimately do with their "divide and conquer" tactic is distort the true purpose of civil rights laws. These laws aren't about preferential treatment; they're about recognizing common, pervasive, and socially injurious forms of discrimination. And whatever the total of injuries that a particular form of discrimination may cost society in the aggregate, for each individual person, the insults to dignity or denials of opportunity she or he experiences are also a world of unique and felt harm that is worth preventing. Gay rights, after all, are nothing more than non-gay rights made available to all.

The freedom-to-marry movement's connection to this country's previous civil rights struggles, then, is about much more than just parallels or analogies. The abolitionist and suffrage movements of the nineteenth century and the racial equality and women's movements of the twentieth century are more than just shining moral moments. They are the wellsprings from which much righteousness in our nation flows, and from which companion social justice movements, including ours, draw. As John Lewis wrote in his memoir, reflecting on the diverse people who put their bodies on the line in a crucial civil rights campaign: "The peace movement, the women's movement, the gay movement—they all have roots that can be traced back to Mississippi in the summer of '64.[34]

And these great and ongoing civil rights struggles are our shared inheritance—and our common mandate—as Americans. And as heirs, each of us has the responsibility to work for the right of all citizens, gay and non-gay, within our communities and in the larger society, to be both different and equal.

We also can and should learn lessons from earlier civil rights battles.

For example, just as 2003 was a pivotal year in the current movement for marriage equality, so 1963 was a landmark year in the civil rights movement for racial equality. And yet, as 1963 dawned, despite the triumph of the Montgomery bus boycott with heroes such as King and Rosa Parks, the galvanizing impact of the Freedom Riders, and the successes in Thurgood Marshall's and the NAACP's legal challenges to Jim Crow laws across the South, including *Brown,* the movement seemed stalled.[35] Rampant segregation and violence remained across the country. The movement's campaign to desegregate Albany, Georgia, had just failed, and three of the groups whose common goal was to fight for the civil rights of African-Americans—the NAACP, the Student Nonviolent Coordinating Committee, and the Southern Christian Leadership Conference—were at odds with each other. What turned 1963 into the milestone year we remember and celebrate?

As Drew Hansen portrays it in his book *The Dream: Martin Luther King, Jr. and the Speech that Inspired a Nation,*[36] I see at least four factors that made the difference:

First, the movement adopted new strategies and embarked on actions that might earlier have seemed too "radical." Most notable was the carefully thought-out decision, accompanied by much organizing in advance and as events proceeded, to "go for broke" in Birmingham, Alabama, considered the "most segregated city in America."

Second, the movement deployed new messengers. In the effort to flood the jails, more and more submitted to arrest, and ultimately King himself went to jail, hoping to galvanize a greater response. The campaign provoked criticism from white allies, including King's fellow clergy—prompting his famous letter—as well as other black leaders, exposing rifts in the civil rights movement documented by Hansen, David Garrow, and other historians.

King demanded too much, even some blacks and some fellow activists said. He didn't allow enough room for compromise, they cried. He came to Birmingham at the wrong time, they complained. The movement was fractious and divided; only in hindsight do we see the civil rights era as linear and assured.

When King's arrest failed to break the back of Birmingham's segregation, the movement sent in kids. New messengers, the children lined up to demonstrate and be arrested, creating images that transformed a watching America's understanding of what was at stake.

And these new messengers and images prompted the third factor: overreaching by the opponents of equality. The tide of kids and the increasing concerns expressed by previously silent moderate voices enraged Sheriff Bull Connor, who unleashed dogs and blasted the nonviolent marchers, including the children, with fire hoses. America's conscience awakened, even as some supportive politicians complained that civil rights was inconveniently crowding out other "issues" they'd rather focus on, "overwhelming the whole program."[37]

Four months later, the movement embarked on yet another new strategic campaign: the celebrated March on Washington. And what most Americans remember more than anything else from that powerful August day is, of course, King's "I Have a Dream" speech. It was a fulfillment of the lesson taught by Hubertine Auclert, a pioneering French suffragist of the nineteenth century. Auclert, the woman who actually coined the word "feminism," instructed, "If you would obtain a right, first you must proclaim it." King's "I Have a Dream" speech transformed the movement and the country, the fourth factor.

In his book, Hansen explains what about that speech was so remarkable, so transformative:

In the year of Birmingham and the murder of Medgar Evers, King somehow persuaded his audience that racial discrimination would one day be no more. This was King's prophetic gift: In order for America to become a truly integrated nation, Americans first needed to be able to envision what that nation would look like. Political argument against segregation was valuable, but it was only a beginning. Imagination, as well as reason, needed to be renewed. By telling the audience of his vision of a nation healed of the sins of racial discrimination, King began the process of bringing that new nation to life—if only, at first, in the minds of his listeners.[38]

By transcending the individual battles of the moment and instead engaging Americans' imagination with previously unthinkable images—such as little black boys and black girls joining hands with little white boys and white girls—King enlarged people's sense of possibilities, offering an empowering vision that made the African-American civil rights struggle a priority for all fair-minded Americans, regardless of race.

Today, the freedom-to-marry campaign also has been bolstered by promising court decisions, by the acts and voices of non-gay and gay elected officials, by the indelible images of couples like Del and Phyllis and the thousands lining up in cities across the country to get married. Like the courts, people are asking why shouldn't we protect all kids, support all families, treat all Americans equally? What is the reason for continuing committed gay couples' exclusion from marriage? Who will be harmed when that discrimination ends?

And while the level of violence and literal disenfranchisement that confronted the racial justice movement at the start of 1963 does not burden the freedom-to-marry movement, we encounter our own obstacles on the road to full equality. As we advance, we need not deny ourselves the benefit of lessons from earlier civil rights battles, the wisdom, passion, and voice, say, in that letter from that Birmingham jail. As some uncomfortable allies urge delay or "compromise"—whether in the form of unequal or barely extant measures such as civil union or domestic partnership—history reminds us that you don't get a full loaf by asking for, or settling for, half. As some react to human rights stands, such as those of Mayor Newsom in San Francisco and Mayor West in New Paltz, by saying we should wait for time or others to bring us the rights we deserve, we have King's words as a caution: "For years now I have heard the word 'Wait!' It rings in the ear of every Negro with piercing familiarity. This 'Wait' has almost always meant 'Never.' "[39]

And we have King's words, too, as an inspiration: "The time is always ripe to do right."[40]

As Americans ask now why marriage equality is important for this country, we, too, can and must together transcend the battles of the day and, instead, share anew our vision of a society finally free of division and discrimination, with equality, liberty, and justice for all.

CHAPTER TEN

WHY THE
FREEDOM TO MARRY
MATTERS TO ME

*Eventually the civil rights movement will have contributed
infinitely more to the nation than the eradication of racial
injustice. It will have enlarged the concept of brotherhood to
a vision of total interrelatedness.*

Martin Luther King Jr. (1963)[1]

*Let us by all means go up, and we shall gain possession of it,
for we shall surely overcome.*

Numbers 13:30

This book has examined the mix of reasons gay and non-gay people have for wanting the freedom to marry—the emotional as well as the economic, the practical as well as the personal, the social as well as the spiritual, the law as well as the love. We've talked about the tangible benefits of marriage, such as Social Security, health care, and protections for kids. And we've talked about the intangible benefits, such as clarity, dignity, and love.

All of these attributes of marriage matter to different people and different couples in different degrees. But the thing that motivates me personally to devote myself to this campaign most of all is the inheritance—the commitment to equality and making the world better—given to all of us by the civil rights leaders who came before. At its core, the freedom-to-marry movement is about the same thing every civil rights struggle has been about: taking seriously our country's promise to be a nation its citizens can make better, its promise to be a place where people don't have to give up their differences or hide them in order to be treated equally.

As someone who served in the Peace Corps and loves to travel, I always return home with a keen sense of gratitude and appreciation for this very precious promise. This country is founded on the idea that we can work within the system to change things—even things that, at the time, seem intractable, perfectly ordered, traditional, and part of "God's plan" (whether that be slavery, women's inequality, or segregation).

Ever since the freedom-to-marry movement began in earnest more than a decade ago in Hawaii, it has provided an opportunity for non-gay people to see the reality and diversity of gay people's lives—to recognize, in the words of the Vermont Supreme Court, our "common humanity." And once people see that common humanity, they also recognize, as the California Supreme Court did when it became the first court to end race discrimination in marriage, that human beings, gay or non-gay, are not "interchangeable as trains." As the court said so long ago, the essence of the freedom to marry is to fall in love with the person of your choice. The court led the country to an understanding that you don't fall in love with a race of people, just as you don't fall in love with a person because he or she is of a particular race. You fall in love with the whole person, and you, as a human being, have the constitutional right, a human right, to marry that person regardless of her or his or your racial background.

Now our society is coming to understand that we, as human beings, don't fall in love with people solely because of their gender, either. Certainly, whether you're gay or non-gay, if you fall in love with a woman, you love her in part because of her gender. But you didn't fall in love with all women, you fell in love with *her*.

Through the examples of same-sex couples who already are getting married (whether in Canada or Massachusetts, San Francisco, Oregon, or New York), and through the freedom-to-marry discussions taking place in courtrooms, conference rooms, and kitchens across the country, society is coming to learn that gay people are no different when it comes to their desire to marry the person of their choice. And once we see that, we also realize that discomfort with change, or the hazy "tradition" so many of us hold so close to our hearts, is actually keeping loving couples from the basic protections and security that so many other Americans cherish and all seek in life. If you're a fair-minded American, you can't help but, in those words of Abraham Lincoln, "think anew."

On June 27, 2003, there were two stories in the *New York Times* of particular interest, and their pairing spoke volumes. The first, the page-one lead story, reported the historic U.S. Supreme Court decision in *Lawrence v. Texas,* repudiating anti-gay discrimination. The second, also on page one, reported the death of the longest-serving member of the U.S. Senate, under the headline, "Strom Thurmond, Senate Institution Who Fought Integration, Dies at 100." Seldom has a newspaper, by simply displaying the day's news side by side, been able to show so powerfully how far our country has come while, at the same time, pointing out how difficult it is to forget where we've been.

Although Strom Thurmond fought at Normandy during World War II, was part of a unit that liberated Nazi war prisoners at Buchenwald, and served as South Carolina's governor and then U.S. senator for a record forty-eight years, he was a political leader on the wrong side of history. And though in later years Thurmond, like George Wallace, repeatedly professed repentance of his discriminatory stands, it is his opposition to integration, his wrong-headed and shameful conduct at a crucial moment in our nation's movement toward equality, for which he will always be remembered.

An obituary like this invites each of us to ask ourselves how *we* will be remembered for our personal acts or silence during this, America's latest fight for equal rights.

Thirty years from now—when gay people have won the freedom to marry and our society looks back and wonders what the big deal was—our children, grandchildren, nieces, and nephews will want to know where we stood and what we did at a pivotal moment. Did we make a difference? Did we stand up for what is right? Or, invoking tradition or our personal religious beliefs, motivated by prejudice or anxiety, hesitant and resistant to change that seemed discomforting, or indifferent to the consequences of our silence and acquiescence, did we turn our backs and deny our fellow human beings liberty, equality, and the pursuit of happiness?

The choice belongs to—just as commitment depends on—each of us. And that is the American way.

Appendix A

Big Questions, Short Answers

Why Does Our Country Need "Gay Marriage"? [1]

We don't. The term "gay marriage" implies that same-sex couples are asking for rights or privileges that married couples do not have, or for something lesser or different. What gay people are seeking is the legal and equal freedom to marry the person they love and care for, just as non-gay Americans do. The Constitution's guarantee of equal protection and the right to marry belongs to us all.

Why Do Same-Sex Couples Need the Right to Marry?

Many committed same-sex couples share the same responsibilities as married couples. However, without the freedom to marry, they do not receive the same recognition or protections for their families as married couples. In fact, same-sex couples and their kids face tremendous discrimination. For example, lesbians and gay men who have been their partner's primary caretaker are often denied hospital visitation when there's been an accident or illness, or the ability to obtain "family" health coverage, or taxation and inheritance rights, or even protection in case the relationship ends. Sometimes they see their children taken away, or their role as parents denied. Regardless of the fact that they have taken responsibility for their children's and their partner's well-being, both economically and emotionally, legally their status is, at best, that of a roommate. Denied the freedom to marry, same-sex couples and their kids are deprived of literally thousands of legal and economic protections and responsibilities, as well as the emotional, social, and spiritual meaning that marriage has for many.

WHY CHANGE THE DEFINITION OF MARRIAGE?

Ending the exclusion of gay people from marriage would not change the "definition" of marriage, but it would remove a discriminatory barrier from the path of people who have made a personal commitment to each other and are now ready and willing to take on the responsibilities and legal commitment of marriage.

This is not the first time our country has struggled over exclusion from and discrimination in marriage. Previous chapters in American history have seen race discrimination in marriage (ended only in 1967), laws making wives legally inferior to husbands (changed as late as the 1970s and 1980s), resistance to allowing people to end failed or abusive marriages through divorce (fought over in the 1940s and 1950s), and even a refusal to allow married and unmarried people to make their own decisions about whether to use contraception or raise children (decided in 1965).

In each of these struggles, opponents of equality claimed that the proposed change was "against the definition of marriage" and "against God's will." Many of the same claims are made today by opponents now seeking to prevent loving same-sex couples from taking on the legal commitment of marriage. Fortunately, our country rejected the "sky is falling" claims of opponents of equality and made marriage a more inclusive and fair commitment of equals. Today we realize that government discrimination in marriage is wrong, and that the choice of a marriage partner belongs to the committed couple, not politicians or pressure groups.

ISN'T MARRIAGE REALLY ABOUT PROCREATION?

No. Many non-gay people marry and cannot or do not have children. And many gay men and lesbians do have children but have been denied the right to raise those children within a marital relationship. Legally and in reality, marriage is best understood as a relationship of emotional and financial interdependence between two people who make a public commitment. Many people wanting to get married—gay or non-gay—wish to be parents; many others do not. The choice belongs to the couple, not the state.

WHAT IF MY RELIGION OPPOSES SAME-SEX RELATIONSHIPS?

This is not about forcing any church to perform or extend religious recognition to any marriages it doesn't want to. This is about the right to the civil marriage license issued by the state, which religious groups should not interfere with (just as the state should not interfere with religious ceremonies one way or the other). Of course, many lesbians and gay men are active in their respective religions, many of which do recognize and support their loving unions and commitments.

WHY AREN'T DOMESTIC PARTNERSHIPS OR CIVIL UNIONS GOOD ENOUGH?

In one state, Vermont, there is now a nonmarriage marital status called "civil union," and other states from California to New Jersey have begun creating new legal relationships to begin providing protections and legal obligations for committed same-sex couples and their kids. Often, in certain municipalities and companies, this limited recognition of relationships between unmarried partners, including same-sex couples, is called "domestic partnership." The legal and economic consequences of such nonmarriage protections vary considerably and are of value to the families covered. However, neither civil unions nor domestic partnerships confer the full security and range of tangible and intangible protections as marriage itself. Such additional forms of recognition are no substitute for the equal right to marry.

Isn't This a Bad Time to Fight for the Right to Marry?

To some, there is never a good time to fight any battle for equal rights. But same-sex couples are lining up by the thousands all across the country seeking marriage licenses, while legislatures and courts are grappling with ending discrimination. Meanwhile, opposition groups for their own political purposes and broader anti-gay, anti-civil-rights, anti-choice, and anti-separation-of-church-and-state agendas, are trying to stampede politicians into denying not just marriage, but any equal protections or recognition for America's gay couples and families. As always in the struggle for human rights, the outcome will depend on how those of us committed to equal rights engage in the state-by-state and national legal and political battles under way and on how many fair-minded (non-gay) Americans speak up against discrimination and division.

How Can I Help?

Whether you are gay or non-gay, you can help by speaking out against discrimination and in favor of equal responsibilities and rights for all Americans. By telling your personal stories and explaining to your family, friends, co-workers, neighbors, and fellow citizens why you cannot remain silent at a crucial civil rights turning-point. By supporting or joining the broad-based coalition of gay and non-gay individuals and groups that support equal marriage rights. By signing on to the Marriage Resolution at www.freedomtomarry.org, and asking others to do the same. By telling politicians, judges, neighbors, and others that it is time to end discrimination throughout the United States.

Appendix B

Discrimination: Protections Denied to Same-Sex Couples and Their Kids

As we have seen, most couples marry for love and the desire to reinforce the personal commitment they have made to each other. Most also want the public statement of commitment and support that marriage offers. The intangible benefits that marriage offers many families include clarity, security, structure, dignity, spiritual significance, and an expectation of permanence, dedication, and stability. Like most non-gay couples, most same-sex couples share these aspirations and needs.

In addition, according to a 2004 report from the U.S. General Accounting Office, there are at least 1,138 tangible benefits, protections, rights, and responsibilities that marriage brings couples and their kids—and that's just at the federal level.[1] Add in state and local law, and the policies of businesses, employers, universities, and other institutions, and it is clear that the denial of marriage to couples and their kids has a substantial impact on every area of life, from raising kids, building a life together, and caring for one another, to retirement, death, and inheritance.[2] Most of these cannot be secured by private agreement or through lawyers.

Here are just some of the ways in which government's denying the freedom to marry punishes couples and families by depriving them of critical tangible as well as intangible protections and responsibilities in virtually every area of life:

◆ Death: If a couple is not married and one partner dies, the other partner is not entitled to get bereavement leave from work, to file wrongful death claims, to draw the Social Security payments of the deceased partner, or to automatically inherit a shared home, assets, or personal items in the absence of a will.

◆ Debts: Unmarried partners do not generally have responsibility for each other's debt.

◆ Divorce: Unmarried couples do not have access to the courts or to the legal and financial guidelines in times of breakup, including rules for how to handle shared property, child support, and alimony, or to protect the weaker party and the kids.

◆ Family leave: Unmarried couples are often not covered by laws and policies that permit people to take medical leave to care for a sick spouse or for the kids.

◆ Health: Unlike spouses, unmarried partners are usually not considered next of kin for the purposes of hospital visitation and emergency medical decisions. In addition, they can't cover their families on their health plans without paying taxes on the coverage, nor are they eligible for Medicare and Medicaid coverage.

◆ Housing: Denied marriage, couples of lesser means are not recognized as a family and thus can be denied or disfavored in their applications for public housing.

◆ Immigration: U.S. residency and family unification are not available to an unmarried partner from another country.

◆ Inheritance: Unmarried surviving partners do not automatically inherit property should their loved one die without a will, nor do they get legal protection for inheritance rights such as elective share or to bypass the hassles and expenses of probate court.

◆ Insurance: Unmarried partners can't always sign up for joint home and auto insurance. In addition, many employers don't cover domestic partners or their biological or nonbiological children in their health insurance plans.

◆ Parenting: Unmarried couples are denied the automatic right to joint parenting, joint adoption, joint foster care, and visitation for nonbiological parents. In addition, the children of unmarried couples are denied the guarantee of child support and an automatic legal relationship to both parents, and are sometimes sent a wrongheaded but real negative message about their own status and family.

◆ Portability: Unlike marriages, which are honored in all states and countries, domestic partnerships and other alternative mechanisms only exist in a few states and countries, are not given any legal acknowledgment in most, and leave families without the clarity and security of knowing what their legal status and rights will be.

◆ Privilege: Unmarried couples are not shielded against having to testify against each other in judicial proceedings, and are also usually denied the coverage in crime-victims counseling and protection programs afforded married couples.

◆ Property: Unmarried couples are excluded from special rules that permit married couples to buy and own property together under favorable terms, rules that protect married couples in their shared homes, and rules regarding the distribution of property in the event of death or divorce.

◆ Retirement: In addition to being denied access to shared or spousal benefits through Social Security as well as coverage under Medicare and other programs, unmarried couples are denied withdrawal rights and protective tax treatment given to spouses with regard to IRAs and other retirement plans.

◆ Taxes: Unmarried couples cannot file joint tax returns and are excluded from tax benefits and claims specific to marriage. In addition, they are denied the right to transfer property to each other and to pool the family's resources without adverse tax consequences.

For more complete lists and illustrations of the thousands of concrete legal and economic family protections and responsibilities for which marriage is the gateway, please see:

◆ Evan Wolfson, "For Richer, For Poorer: Same-Sex Couples and the Freedom to Marry as a Civil Right," June 2003, http://www.freedomtomarry.org/resources_new.asp?node=58 (denial of marriage harms the most vulnerable, including people of lesser means, people who are ill, immigrants, and children)

◆ Fact sheets and publications from various Freedom to Marry partner organizations: http://www.freedomtomarry.org/national_partners.asp?doc_id=1025

APPENDIX C

GETTING INVOLVED

It is an axiom of social change that no revolution can take place without a methodology suited to the circumstances of the period.

Martin Luther King Jr. (1963)[1]

Put a human face on it. Let's not talk about it in theory. Give me a story. Give me lives.

San Francisco Mayor Gavin Newsom (2004)[2]

When Massachusetts lawmakers gathered in February 2004 to begin a constitutional convention that anti-gay forces hoped would circumvent the state high court ruling ordering an end to discrimination in marriage, state Representative Elizabeth Malia decided it was time to put a human face on the debate. She wanted to remind her colleagues that she is a lesbian and that their decision would have a direct effect on her life and on her family's welfare. After conceding that she isn't "the most eloquent speaker, or one of the great minds of this House," she proceeded to open her heart to her fellow legislators, explaining, "There is no way for those of us in the gay and lesbian community to convey the reality of our lives unless we tell you about them." Malia then told her fellow legislators about her partner of thirty years, Rita, and described her own fear of dying early and how Rita would be left without any of the protections provided married spouses at such times of loss. "I ask you, please, to look into your hearts," she said. "I understand that's not a possibility for everyone." [3]

Difficult as it may have been for Malia to be so open about her personal life, it was clear how successful she was in persuading at least one colleague, Republican Representative Shaun P. Kelly, to open his eyes to the needs of gay and lesbian couples and their families. Malia and Kelly are political opposites, but they are friends. And as Kelly rose to address his colleagues, he said he could not, in good conscience, vote for any legislation that limited her civil rights.

"Liz, this is for you," Kelly said as he began his speech. "Enshrining in the constitution a document under which [Malia] leaves the chamber and doesn't have the privileges that other people have cannot possibly jibe with what the constitution and democracy is all about." [4]

"If you believe the love that Liz has for her partner is less than the love you have for your spouse, I would suggest that you're wrong," he added. "You would never say you were superior to the gentlelady from Jamaica Plain. You wouldn't do it. You wouldn't say that to her face." [5]

Later, during an interview with the *Boston Globe,* Kelly explained,

> My colleagues probably would say they love Liz and admire Liz and respect Liz. So I thought, would they really then turn around and vote to enshrine in this document language that keeps Liz as a permanent second-class citizen? I thought it was the best and most appropriate and maybe the most meaningful

way to sort of have people look at this from a little bit of a different perspective.[6]

Representative Cory Atkins, who told the *Boston Phoenix* that she was so overcome by Kelly's speech that she "was shaking and crying," added, "I didn't see how after that speech anyone could have voted against Liz."[7]

Of course there were people who voted against Liz Malia. In fact, only forty-four legislators supported Kelly's motion to immediately end the constitutional convention out of respect for Massachusetts's gay and lesbian legislators, let alone the gay families throughout the state and nation. Nevertheless, as Malia told colleagues about her life and, in turn, inspired Kelly to break away from his fellow Republicans and speak so movingly in favor of the civil rights of his political opposite, the power of speaking out—of telling your own story—was never more obvious.

That's why, when people ask me how they can get involved in the freedom-to-marry campaign, my first request is they do just what Representatives Malia and Kelly did: tell their stories. However, you don't have to be gay or lesbian, like Liz Malia—or even have a gay or lesbian friend or family member, as did Shaun Kelly—to have a story that's worth telling. You only have to be an American who takes the Constitution and this country's commitment to equality seriously. Or for that matter, you only have to be a compassionate conservative who believes in treating others as you would want to be treated.

As you know, America has already made great strides toward marriage equality, but this is a crucial time, a civil rights moment. In the years that I have been working to end discrimination in marriage, my mantra traveling around the country has been "There is no marriage without engagement." All of us who care need to engage our family, friends, neighbors, co-workers, and fellow citizens, asking them to take a deep breath, think it through, and stand up for what is right—and diverse stories, compelling messengers, and the personal ask are what make the difference.

By adding your story and your ask to those already out there, you help other people realize this debate is not about nothing, not about hypotheticals, and not about someone they don't know. It helps them realize that the freedom-to-marry movement is about their friends, neighbors, co-workers, and fellow congregants—and about you, because you matter to them and you care.

Since you've already taken the time to read this book, you probably already realize how important your voice is. Your participation in this movement, at this moment, will make a difference. With that in mind, I've listed a number of ways you can contribute to this campaign:

♦ Talk with other people about gay people and marriage equality using resources such as materials on www.freedomto marry.org and the "Big Questions, Short Answers" found in Appendix A. Many people do not realize that prohibitions against same-sex couples marrying are discriminatory. Others need to hear that there is a difference between religious ceremonies and governmental and civil marriage and be reassured that different faiths and congregations will still be able to handle religious marriage as they see fit.

♦ Again, hearing the stories of real people—how marriage would make a difference in their everyday lives—is perhaps the most effective way to help people understand marriage equality. In other words, they may not even realize that the denial of the freedom to marry directly concerns someone they know. You are the story they need to hear!

◆ Write to family and friends telling them why you care about marriage equality, and asking them to care, too. A good example of such a letter, and the response it got, was written by a gay man at the *Advocate* and can be found at http://www.advocate .com/html/stories/911/911_letter.asp.

◆ Educate yourself with the information available from many wonderful organizations, gay and non-gay, working together to secure marriage equality. A good starting point is the resources and links to be found on Freedom to Marry's Web site, www.freedomtomarry.org.

◆ Contact your national elected representatives, urging them to support marriage equality and asking them to defend against any attempts to amend the U.S. Constitution (or to otherwise legislate inequality). Closer to home, write, call, e-mail, or fax your state elected representatives, letting them know you will not stand for discrimination when it comes to marriage rights. If officials you know already support marriage equality, write to them anyway, thank them for their support, and offer to be a resource to them as they continue their work on our behalf. To prepare yourself, visit the Web sites of supportive non-gay groups such as People for the American Way, www.pfaw.org, or the National Organization for Women, www.now.org; gay organizations such as the Human Rights Campaign, www.hrc .org, the Log Cabin Republicans, www.lcr.org, or the National Gay and Lesbian Task Force, www.thetaskforce.org, or www .Congress.org. Many such groups provide easy ways to contact your elected officials. The last Web site can even help you identify state and local representatives simply by keying in your ZIP code.

◆ Get to know your statewide political advocacy organization, national and local gay and lesbian civil rights organizations, and any other groups working together to end marriage discrimination. You can find a list of these groups at Freedom to Marry's Web site, www.freedomtomarry.org. Many of these groups provide ongoing information, alerts about breaking news that affects you, speaker trainings, community forums, and more. There is a range of ways to participate—out front or behind the scenes—and both statewide and national organizations especially need volunteers, donations, and people who will participate in storytelling, letter writing, and other positive actions.

◆ Create a visibility event in your neighborhood, in your workplace, on campus, or within an organization by distributing information about the need for marriage equality.

◆ Ask someone you know—or everyone you know—to get engaged in the campaign by circulating and signing the Marriage Resolution at http://www.freedomtomarry.org/marriage_reso lution.asp.

◆ Write a letter to the editor of your local newspaper—or another publication—in support of marriage equality for same-sex couples. Use the opportunity to positively address recent news coverage of the marriage-equality movement. If the publication in question has not carried recent coverage of the topic, you may want to make your letter timelier—and therefore more likely to be published—by mentioning proposed legislation or litigation, news events that relate to the subject, and so on.

◆ Sign up for the regular updates on the marriage-equality movement by joining the mailing list at www.freedomtomarry .org. Invite your friends and family to do the same.

◆ Write to a newspaper, magazine, TV station, radio station, or some other media outlet urging them to cover marriage equality. If you are willing, serve as a resource for them, agreeing to be interviewed or helping to find people who will talk to a reporter about the subject. Provide the media outlet with information about organizations they might talk to for their coverage of the issue. To prepare yourself, check out the resources on the Web site of the Gay & Lesbian Alliance Against Defamation, www.glaad.org.

◆ Write an article or op-ed piece for your local paper or a publication affiliated with an organization in which you're involved, such as a labor union newsletter or a denominational newspaper. Find out the publication's guidelines and write about marriage equality, what it means to you, and why you think it should matter to other people. Your story will help personalize the issue, which always helps others to learn about a subject (even if you think they're opposed.)

◆ Ask your clergy, local business or union leaders, elected officials, your favorite celebrity, an athlete you admire, or other high-profile opinion leaders to sign the Marriage Resolution and become one of Freedom to Marry's Voices of Equality, a diverse group of Americans speaking out in support of marriage equality for same-sex couples.

◆ Host or sponsor a house party, to which you can invite family and friends to learn about marriage equality and how they can help support a local group and actions or a member of the coalition. Use your house party as a chance to talk candidly with neighbors, elected officials, and members of the media about marriage equality.

◆ Host or sponsor a family picnic for gay and lesbian families and allies and invite the neighborhood, the media, and elected officials. Provide them with information about marriage equality and ask them to work with you toward achieving this civil right. You'll be profiling the real families and lives at the heart of this struggle.

◆ Working with a local group, invite the media to cover the couples seeking to marry—and facing discrimination—at the local marriage license bureau. When same-sex couples apply for a marriage license, it often makes news. In most cases, the right to apply for a marriage license will be denied. Really make the moment count by using it as a concrete example of the lack of marriage equality. If you have members of the media with you, they can tell the story of efforts toward marriage equality through your personal story or your friends' stories. The Metropolitan Community Church Web site, www.mccchurch.org, for example, provides a kit that may help you organize such actions.

◆ Share your story with groups like Freedom to Marry, the American Civil Liberties Union (www.aclu.org), or Parents, Families and Friends of Lesbians and Gays (www.pflag.org). In one hundred words or less, and within the body text of an e-mail, tell us your story, providing your contact information and letting us know whether we can share your stories with others—including the media.

◆ Engage communities of faith in your work toward marriage equality. As you know, religious and spiritual leaders have a special role to play in the marriage-equality movement, both by clarifying the important difference between civil and religious marriage and by speaking up for love and equality under law. Ask your faith leaders to hold a special service about marriage equality or to speak out on the subject. Ask your clergy if they will present a sermon or talk about the issue. Help them make your faith community a place for everyone. Make sure your faith community and its newsletters and programs are a source of information on marriage equality for same-sex couples.

Just as we all have different stories to share, all of us also have different ways to share them. There is no one action that fits all. When going through the list above, consider what you're most comfortable doing. If you're not comfortable joining a group, consider devoting your time to a personal letter-writing campaign. On the other hand, if you prefer to work behind the scenes, consider contacting one of the groups listed on the Freedom to Marry Web site and find out how you can help support one of their marriage-equality actions.

Keep in mind that it's okay to start small. Choose to talk first with your friends and family before moving out in expanding concentric circles. And when writing letters, whether to your family, friends, and co-workers or to politicians, remember that e-mail is important, but much less effective than personal meetings, phone calls, faxes, or letters.

You don't have to reinvent the wheel in order to make a difference. This movement may be relatively new to you—and it will probably be more new to many of the people you speak with—but there are plenty of tools and support available through participating gay and non-gay groups across the country. Again, you can find a list of these groups at www.freedomtomarry.org. And, again, most of them involve non-gay and gay Americans working together. Everyone is welcome, and needed.

Most important, remember the power of your own voice. Like Liz Malia, you might not consider yourself one of the most "eloquent voices" or "greatest minds" in your house. But just as Representative Malia showed when she addressed her colleagues in the Massachusetts Legislature, nothing can change more minds or sway more hearts than personal conviction in the name of civil rights, and the bravery to speak out and tell your own story.

As President Kennedy said in his crucial address to the nation on civil rights, just a few months before his assassination, "The heart of the question is whether all Americans are to be afforded equal rights and equal opportunities. . . . Those who do nothing are inviting shame and violence. Those who act boldly are recognizing right as well as reality."[8]

Marriage matters. And so does what we do to help make a better world.

APPENDIX D

WORKING TOGETHER

Here are the Web sites for many of the gay and non-gay organizations, national and state, working together for marriage equality. Please visit the ones that work best for you, or access them all through the Freedom to Marry Web site, www.freedomtomarry .org, which also contains additional contact information (addresses, phone numbers) and ways to get involved.

NATIONAL

AMERICAN CIVIL LIBERTIES UNION (ACLU)
  www.aclu.org
CHILDREN OF LESBIANS AND GAYS EVERYWHERE (COLAGE)
  www.colage.org
DONTAMEND.COM
  www.dontamend.com
EGALE CANADA
  www.egale.ca
FAMILY PRIDE COALITION
  www.familypride.org
FREEDOM TO MARRY
  www.freedomtomarry.org
GAY & LESBIAN ADVOCATES & DEFENDERS (GLAD)
  www.glad.org

Gay & Lesbian Alliance Against Defamation
(GLAAD)
www.glaad.org

Gay & Lesbian Victory Fund
www.victoryfund.org

Human Rights Campaign (HRC)
www.hrc.org

Lambda Legal Defense & Education Fund
(Lambda Legal)
www.lambdalegal.org

Log Cabin Republicans
www.logcabin.org

National Black Justice Coalition
www.nbjcoalition.org

National Center for Lesbian Rights (NCLR)
www.nclrights.org

National Gay and Lesbian Task Force
(The Task Force)
www.thetaskforce.org

National Latina/o Lesbian, Gay, Bisexual &
Transgender Organization (LLEGO)
www.llego.org

National Organization for Women (NOW)
www.now.org

Parents, Families and Friends of Lesbians and
Gays (PFLAG)
www.pflag.org

People For the American Way
www.pfaw.org

Soulforce
www.soulforce.org

UNIVERSAL FELLOWSHIP OF METROPOLITAN COMMUNITY
   CHURCHES (MCC)
   www.mccchurch.org

STATE

CALIFORNIA

CALIFORNIA FREEDOM TO MARRY COALITION
   www.civilmarriage.org

EQUALITY CALIFORNIA
   www.eqca.org

MARRIAGE EQUALITY CALIFORNIA (MECA)
   www.marriageequalityca.org

COLORADO

CIVIL RIGHTS NOW:
   www.civilrightsnow.org

CONNECTICUT

LOVE MAKES A FAMILY
   www.lmfct.org

FLORIDA

EQUALITY FLORIDA
   www.equalityflorida.org

GEORGIA

GEORGIA EQUALITY
   www.georgiaequality.org

MARYLAND

EQUALITY MARYLAND
   www.equalitymaryland.org

MASSACHUSETTS

FREEDOM TO MARRY COALITION OF MASSACHUSETTS
   www.equalmarriage.org

GLAD
    www.glad.org

MassEquality
    www.massequality.org

Religious Coalition for the Freedom to Marry
    www.ftmmass.org/rcfm

MICHIGAN

Triangle Foundation
    www.tri.org

MINNESOTA

Outfront Minnesota
    www.outfront.org

MISSISSIPPI

Equality Mississippi
    www.equalityms.org

NEW HAMPSHIRE

New Hampshire Freedom to Marry
    www.nhftm.org

GLAD
    www.glad.org

NEW JERSEY

Lambda Legal
    www.lambdalegal.org

NEW YORK

Empire State Pride Agenda
    www.prideagenda.org

Marriage Equality New York
    www.marriageequalityny.org

The Wedding Party
    www.theweddingparty.org

NORTH CAROLINA

SOUTHERNERS ON NEW GROUND (SONG)
www.southnewground.org

OREGON

BASIC RIGHTS OREGON
www.basicrights.org

PENNSYLVANIA

CENTER FOR LESBIAN AND GAY CIVIL RIGHTS
www.center4civilrights.org

SOUTH CAROLINA

SOUTH CAROLINA GAY AND LESBIAN PRIDE MOVEMENT
www.scglpm.org

UTAH

EQUALITY UTAH
www.equalityutah.org

VERMONT

VERMONT FREEDOM TO MARRY TASK FORCE
www.vtfreetomarry.org

WASHINGTON

LEGAL MARRIAGE ALLIANCE OF WASHINGTON
www.lmaw.org

PARTNERS TASK FORCE FOR GAY & LESBIAN COUPLES
www.buddybuddy.com

WISCONSIN

ACTION WISCONSIN
www.actionwisconsin.org

Notes

Epigraphs

1. Abraham Lincoln, "Letters to Henry L. Pierce and Others (April 6, 1859)," in *The Collected Works of Abraham Lincoln,* ed. Roy P. Basler (Piscataway, N.J.: Rutgers University Press, 1953), p. 376.

2. *United States v. Virginia,* 116 S. Ct. 2264, 2287 (U.S. Supreme Court, 1996). See also *Lawrence v. Texas,* No. 02-102 (U.S. Supreme Court, 2003): ("As the Constitution endures, persons in every generation can invoke its principles in their own search for greater freedom.")

3. Suzan Clarke, "Speakers Discuss Impact of Gay-Marriage Ban," *White Plains (N.Y.) Journal News,* March 29, 2004, http://www.thejournalnews.com/newsroom/032904/b0129stonewall.html.

One: What Is Marriage?

1. *Goodridge v. Department of Public Health,* 440 Mass. 309 (Massachusetts Supreme Judicial Court, 2003).

2. For a fuller list, please see Appendix B.

3. Hendrik Hartog, "What Gay Marriage Teaches About the History of Marriage," History News Network, April 5, 2004, http://hnn.us/articles/4400.html (lecture by author of *Man and Wife in America: A History* to Organization of American Historians tracing evolution of marriage and past battles).

4. Andrew Jacobs, "More Than Mere Partners, *New York Times,* December 19, 2003, p. B1.

5. "New Black Group to Fight for Marriage Equality," *Blacklight,* National Black Justice Coalition, March 24, 2004, http://www.blacklightonline.com/fma.html.

6. David Cray, "Painful Choices Face Many Same-sex Couples When One is American, the Other Foreign," Associated Press, November 23, 2003.

7. Cray, "Painful Choices."

8. John Chadwick, "White House Working on Law to Block Gay Marriage," *Bergen County (N.J.) Record,* July 31, 2003, p. A1.

9. Lambda Legal, "New Jersey Family Profiles," March 24, 2004, http://www.lambdalegal.org/cgibin/iowa/documents/record?record=1068.

10. Evan Thomas, "The War Over Gay Marriage," *Newsweek,* July 7, 2003, p. 38.

11. Richard Jerome, "State of the Union," *People,* August 18, 2003, p. 100.

Two: Why Now?

1. Martin Luther King Jr., "Seventh Annual Gandhi Memorial Lecture," Howard University, Washington, D.C., November 6, 1966.

2. Ann Davidson, "At Long Last! Ben and Greg are Married," *San Jose Mercury News,* March 17, 2004.

3. "Transcript of the Mark-Up Record of the Defense of Marriage Act, House Judiciary Committee, June 12, 1996," in *Same-Sex Marriage, Pro and Con: A Reader,* ed. Andrew Sullivan (New York: Vintage, 1977), pp. 222–24.

4. "Transcript of the Mark-Up Record," pp. 223–24.

5. Martin Luther King Jr., "Letter from a Birmingham Jail," in *Why We Can't Wait* (New York: Harper & Row, 1964), pp. 79, 85.

6. *Gay & Lesbian Alliance Against Defamation,* 24 March 2004, http://www.glaad.org/action/campaigns_detail.php?id=3296; see also "Washington Post Weddings Section Prints First Same-Sex Wedding Announcement," July 23, 2003. After the *Washington Post* printed the announcement of her June 27, 2003, Toronto wedding to syndicated columnist Deb Price, journalist Joyce Murdoch remarked, "We are lawfully married, thanks to Canada. And *The Washington Post* should be heartily applauded for recognizing that simple reality and for showing us exactly the same respect it has always given married couples."

7. *Lawrence v. Texas,* No. 02-102 (U.S. Supreme Court, 2003) (Scalia, J., dissenting).

8. Human Rights Campaign, "HRC Releases Poll Data Showing Plurality of Americans Support or Accept Marriage Rights for Gay and Lesbian Cou-

ples," Peter D. Hart Research Associates and American Viewpoint, August 1, 2003 (on file with author).

9. President George W. Bush, State of the Union address to Congress, January 20, 2004.

10. Patricia Leigh Brown, "For Children of Gays, Marriage Brings Joy," *New York Times,* March 19, 2004.

11. Frank Rich, "The Joy of Gay Marriage," *New York Times,* February 29, 2004, sec. 2, p. 1.

12. Elaine Herscher, "When Marriage is a Tough Proposal," *San Francisco Chronicle,* May 15, 1995, p. A1.

13. Carol Ness, "Marriage Made in Heaven Hellishly Hard to Legalize," *San Francisco Examiner,* April 27, 1994, p. A1.

14. Robin Clark, "Gay Rights Flourish in Hawaii's Climate," *Philadelphia Inquirer,* August 30, 1994, p. A1.

15. Susan Essoyan, "Hawaiian Wedding Bells Ring Alarm Bells," *Los Angeles Times,* September 8, 1996, p. A1.

16. Lambda Legal, "Counsel in Landmark Hawaii Marriage Case Is Named Judge," August 7, 2000, http://www.lambdalegal.org/cgi-bin/iowa/doc uments/record?record=668.

17. Bruce Vilanch, "25 Coolest Straight People," *Advocate,* November 10, 1998.

18. Lambda Legal, "Counsel in Landmark Hawaii Marriage Case."

19. *Baehr v. Lewin,* 852 P.2d 44 (Hawaii Supreme Court, 1993).

20. See, e.g., Evan Wolfson, "Civil Rights, Human Rights, Gay Rights: Minorities and the Humanity of the Different," *Harvard Journal of Law and Public Policy* 14(1991):22.

21. Donald Kaul, http://www.qrd.org/qrd/world/wockner/quote.unquote/059=02.20.96

22. George de Lama, "Hawaii May Lead Way on Same-Sex Marriage," *Chicago Tribune,* May 15, 1994, p. 21.

23. *Crossfire,* CNN, May 19, 1993.

24. James Kunen, "Hawaiian Courtship," *Time,* December 16, 1996, p. 44.

25. *Nightline,* ABC, September 25, 1995.

26. Ed Fallon, "I Have Anguished," speech to Iowa House of Representatives, February 20, 1996.

27. Joan C. Callahan, "Testimony Before the Joint House and Senate Judiciary Committee," Kentucky statehouse, Frankfort, August 19, 1997.

28. National Gay and Lesbian Task Force, "Statement on ENDA and DOMA," September 10, 1996, http://www.thetaskforce.org/news/release.cfm?releaseID=178.

29. John Lewis, "A Mean Bill," speech to U.S. House of Representatives, Washington, D.C., July 11, 1996.

30. *Baehr v. Miike,* 994 P.2d 566 (Hawaii Supreme Court, 1999).

31. *Turner v. Safley,* 482 U.S. 78 (U.S. Supreme Court, 1987).

32. Carey Goldberg, "Hawaii Judge Ends Gay-Marriage Ban," *New York Times,* December 4, 1996, p. A1.

33. *Baehr v. Miike.*

34. *Baker v. Vermont,* 774 A.2d 864 (Vermont Supreme Court, 1999).

35. *Goodridge v. Department of Public Health,* 440 Mass. 309 (Massachusetts Supreme Judicial Court, 2003).

36. Frederick Douglass, "West India Emancipation," speech delivered at Canadaigua, New York, August 4, 1857, in *The Life and Writings of Frederick Douglass,* vol. 2, ed. Philip S. Foner (New York: International Publishers, 1950), p. 437.

37. "As our case is new, so we must think anew, and act anew. We must disenthrall ourselves, and then we shall save our country" (Abraham Lincoln, "Second Annual Message to Congress," U.S. Capitol, Washington, D.C., December 1, 1862).

38. Christy Harvey, "Optimism Outduels Pessimism," *Wall Street Journal,* Sept. 16, 1999, p. A10.

Three: Will Allowing Gay Couples to Marry Harm Society?

1. American Center for Law & Justice, "In Defense of Marriage," pp. 4–5 (1997).

2. Ike Awgu, "Gay Marriage Opposition Has Ugly Ancestry," *Ottawa Sun,* February 18, 2004, p. 13.

3. *Good Morning America,* ABC, November 19, 2003.

4. E. J. Graff, *What Is Marriage For? The Strange Social History of Our Most Intimate Institution* (Boston: Beacon Press, 1999), p. 24.

5. Graff, *What Is Marriage For?* p. 27.

6. Lara Jakes Jordan, "With Eye on Leadership, Santorum Policy, Politics Driven by Family," Associated Press, April 20, 2003.

7. Chris Bull, "Why It's Still OK to be Antigay," *Advocate,* June 10, 2003.

8. Eric Zorn, "Marriage Issue Just as Plain as Black and White," *Chicago Tribune,* May 19, 1996.

9. Graff, *What Is Marriage For?* pp. 231–33.

10. Quoted in Graff, *What Is Marriage For?* p. 239.

11. Graff, *What Is Marriage For?* p. 237.

12. Graff, *What Is Marriage For?* p. 237.

13. Kenneth J. Parsigian, "Amici Curiae Brief of the Professors of the History of Marriage, Families, and the Law," *Goodridge v. Department of Public Health* (Massachusetts Supreme Judicial Court, 2003).

14. Graff, *What Is Marriage For?* pp. 30–31.

15. Graff, *What Is Marriage For?* pp. 32–33.

16. Parsigian, "Amici Curiae Brief."

17. David Garrow, *Liberty and Sexuality: The Right to Privacy and the Making of Roe v. Wade* (New York: Macmillan, 1994), pp. 27, 108.

18. *Griswold v. Connecticut,* 31 U.S. 479 (U.S. Supreme Court, 1965).

19. Nancy F. Cott, *Public Vows: A History of Marriage and the Nation* (Cambridge, Mass.: Harvard University Press, 2000), pp. 40–44.

20. *Scott v. Georgia,* 39 Ga. 321, 323 (Georgia Supreme Court, 1869) (forbidding marriage between a French man and a black woman).

21. *Federalist* 78.

22. *Perez v. Sharp,* 198 P.2d 17, 25 (Cal. 1948).

23. Deb Price, "Civil Rites: Arguments Against Same-Sex Marriage Mirror Those That Kept the Races Apart," *Detroit News,* April 18, 1997.

24. *Loving v. Virginia,* 388 U.S. 1 (U.S. Supreme Court, 1967).

25. *New York Times,* November 10, 1958 (U.S. ranked last in interracial Gallup survey of attitudes toward interracial marriage, with 72 percent of Americans still disapproving, a year and a half after *Loving v. Virginia.*

26. Ramesh Ponnuru, "Coming Out Ahead: Why Gay Marriage Is on the Way," *National Journal,* July 28, 2003.

FOUR: ISN'T MARRIAGE FOR PROCREATION?

1. *Fox News Sunday,* Fox News Network, August 3, 2003.

2. *Goodridge v. Department of Public Health,* 440 Mass. 309 (Massachusetts Supreme Judicial Court, 2003).

3. "Talking Points Against Same-Sex Marriage," *Point of View* radio talk show, *Christianity.com* http://www.pointofview.net/partner/Article_Display_Page/0_PTID320166%7CCHID644214%7CCIID1690590.00.html.

4. Matthew Johnson, "Lily Pads/Pink Flowers: Gay Marriage, Hawaii Sovereignty, and Justice for All in Paradise," http://www.gwu.edu/~english/ccsc/2002%20Pages/Johnson.htm; see also Robert J. Morris, "Configuring the Bounds of Marriage: The Implications of Hawaiian Culture and Values for the Debate About Homogamy," *Yale Journal of Law and the Humanities* 8 (1996): 132–57.

5. Closing argument by Hawaii Deputy State Attorney General Rick Eichor, *Baehr v. Miike* (Hawaii Supreme Court, September 1996).

6. "Vermont Gay Couples Tell Court Why They Should Be Allowed to Marry," *CNN.com,* November 18, 1998, http://www.cnn.com/US/9811/18/gay.marriage.03.

7. "Supreme Court Considers Gay Marriage Case," *Out in the Mountains,* December 1998, http://www.mountainpridemedia.org/dec98/court.htm.

8. M. R. F. Buckley, "State's High Court Debates Gay Marriage," *TheBostonChannel.com,* November 19, 2003, http://www.thebostonchannel.com/news/2645605/detail.htm.

9. *Baehr v. Miike,* 994 P.2d 566 (Hawaii Supreme Court, 1999).

10. *Baker v. Vermont,* 774 A.2d 864 (Vermont Supreme Court, 1999).

11. Buckley, "State's High Court Debates Gay Marriage."

12. *Lawrence v. Texas,* No. 02-102 (U.S. Supreme Court, 2003) (Scalia, J., dissenting).

13. *Eisenstadt v. Baird,* 405 U.S. 438 (U.S. Supreme Court, 1972).

14. *Fox News Sunday,* Fox News Network, August 3, 2003.

15. Bruce Dunford, "Absent Fireworks, Gay Marriage Trial Focuses on Parenting," Associated Press, September 15, 1996.

16. Jerome Richard, "State of the Union," *People,* August 18, 2003, p. 100.

17. Gay & Lesbian Advocates & Defenders, "GLAD—Marriage in Massachusetts," http://www.glad.org/marriage/goodridge_plaintiffs.shtml.

18. University of Massachusetts at Amherst, "UMass Study of Census Data Shows that 8,000 Massachusetts Children with Same-Sex Parents Would Greatly Benefit from Gay Marriage," news release, February 9, 2004, http://www.umass.edu/newsoffice/archive/2004/020904iglss.html.

19. Urban Institute/Human Rights Campaign analysis, March 2004, http://www.hrc.org.

20. Michael S. Wald, "Same-Sex Couples: Marriage, Families, and Children," *BuddyBuddy.com,* December 1999, http://www.buddybuddy.com/wald1 .html.

Five: What About the Children?

1. *Baker v. Vermont,* 744 A.2d 864 (Vermont Supreme Court, 1999).

2. *Religion & Ethics Newsweekly,* WNET-TV, New York, N.Y., January 16, 2004.

3. See, e.g., Urban Institute/Human Rights Campaign analysis, March 2004, http://www.hrc.org/Content/ContentGroups/Publications1/marriage booklet03192004.pdf; see also National Gay and Lesbian Task Force, "The 2000 Census and Same-Sex Households," http://www.thetaskforce.org/downloads/census/CensusFull.pdf.

4. "Gay Men Lose Challenge to Adoption Ban," Associated Press, January 29, 2004.

5. Elisabeth J. Beardsley, "Pols Seeking 'Rational' Way Around Gay Marriage Ruling," *Boston Herald,* January 14, 2004.

6. Maggie Gallagher, "The Stakes," *National Review Online,* July 14, 2003, http://www.nationalreview.com/comment/comment-gallagher071403.asp.

7. Brian S. Brown, "Same-Sex Marriage Is a Symptom of Cultural Decline," *Hartford Courant,* February 9, 2004.

8. See, for example, http://www.thetaskforce.org/marriagecenter/Mar riageProtectionWeek.pdf. (The Web sites of the nine right-wing groups surveyed mentioned *homosexual* in 2,369 documents, compared to 841 such mentions for *divorce,* 832 for *poverty,* 207 for *health insurance,* 190 for *domestic violence,* and only 85 for *child support.*)

9. Greg Barrett, "In Gay Households, Familiar Endearments Acquire New Meaning," *Arizona Republic,* April 11, 2004.

10. Andrew E. Cherlin, Frank F. Furstenberg, Sara S. McLanahan, Gary

D. Sandefur, and Lawrence L. Wu, "Brief of Amici Curiae," *Baehr v. Miike* (Hawaii Supreme Court, December 11, 1996).

11. Cherlin et al., "Brief of Amici Curiae."

12. Michael S. Wald, "Same-Sex Couples: Marriage, Families, and Children," *BuddyBuddy.com,* December 1999, http://www.buddybuddy.com/wald1.html.

13. Wald, "Same-Sex Couples."

14. Wald, "Same-Sex Couples."

15. Wald, "Same-Sex Couples."

16. Quoted in Wald, "Same-Sex Couples."

17. Human Rights Campaign Foundation, "Professional Opinion," http://www.hrc.org/template.cfm?Section=Parenting&Contentid=14091&template=/contentmanagement/contentdisplay.cfm.

18. "Coparent or Second-Parent Adoption by Same-Sex Parents," *Pediatrics,* February 2002, pp. 339–40.

19. Family Pride Coalition, "Myths and Facts," 2002, http://www.familypride.org/issues/myths.htm.

20. Ronald Reagan, "Two Ill-Advised California Trends," *Los Angeles Herald-Examiner,* November 1, 1978, p. A-19.

21. Jessica Portner, "Homosexual Students: A Group Particularly Vulnerable to Suicide," *Education Week,* April 19, 2000.

22. Rory Schuler, "Trial in Teen's Suicide Targets Three Police Officers," *Pottsville (Pa.) Republican & Evening Herald,* November 6, 2001.

23. Damon R. Dillman, "Family, Friends Pay Tribute to Wayman," *Pottsville (Pa.) Republican & Evening Herald,* November 18, 2002.

24. Dillman, "Family, Friends Pay Tribute."

25. To give one example, as one expert on marriage and partnership in Scandinavia reports: "It is interesting to note that, in Scandinavia, just as in the U.S., those on the right predicted that passage of gay marriage legislation would lead to the downfall of the institution of marriage. However, in looking at statistics from the 1990s, we see that in the years after the passage of gay marriage legislation in Denmark, the rates of heterosexual marriage went *up,* and the rates of heterosexual divorce went *down,* completely contrary to the predictions of conservatives. In 1990, at the outset of the partnership law's existence, there were 6.1 heterosexual marriages per 1,000 persons in Denmark. By the mid-1990's (1996), that number had climbed to 6.8 marriages per 1,000 population, or an

increase of just over 10% from 1990. Furthermore, the number of heterosexual divorces in 1990 stood at 2.7 per 1,000 population. By the mid-1990's, it was at 2.4 per 1,000, or an approximate 12% decrease in the number of divorces." (Darren R. Spedale, manuscript with author, March 2004, pp. 4–5.

26. To give just two examples: A *Catholic World*/UCLA comparative survey published in March 2003 showed 77 percent of Catholic high school seniors in secular schools and 69 percent in parochial schools supported same-sex couples' freedom to marry, with a significant increase in support from freshman to senior year. And in a September 2003 Gallup/*USA Today*/CNN poll, 67 percent of those under 30 years old and 53 percent of those 30–49 said that ending the denial of marriage to same-sex couples would have a net positive effect on society.

Six: Isn't Marriage a Religious Matter?

1. Mark Thiessen, "Mormons Told Stable Homes Are Safe Havens from Moral Disease," Associated Press, April 4, 2004.

2. John F. Kennedy, "Address to the Greater Houston Ministerial Association," Houston, September 12, 1960.

3. Unitarian Universalist Association, "Religious Coalition for the Freedom to Marry Meets at UUA Headquarters," February 5, 2004, http://www.uua.org/news/2004/freedomtomarry/040205=rcfm.html.

4. "Vatican Drive to Curb Gay Marriage," July 21, 2003, BBC News, http://news.bbc.co.uk/2/hi/europe/3108349.stm.

5. "Mormon Leader Blasts Same-Sex Marriage," Associated Press, August 20, 2003.

6. Michael Paulson, "Jewish Group OK's Same-Sex Marriage," *Boston Globe,* January 16, 2004.

7. Peter J. Gomes, "Moral Imagination, Gay Marriage, and the Right Thing for Massachusetts," speech at Massachusetts Statehouse, Boston, February 10, 2004.

8. David D. Kirkpatrick, "Gay Marriage Fight Finds Ambivalence From Evangelicals," *New York Times,* February 28, 2004.

9. David Van Biema, "Mainline Churches: Not Quite as Liberal as They Look," *Time,* February 9, 2004.

10. Matthew 22:21.

NOTES

11. Michael Paulson, "Bishops Try to Mobilize on Marriage," *Boston Globe,* January 17, 2004.

12. Bob Egelko, "Proposed Gay Marriage Ban Splits Religious Community," Associated Press, March 3, 2000.

13. Egelko, "Proposed Gay Marriage Ban."

14. Mark Pratt, "Catholic Mass Disturbed After Anti-Gay Marriage Video Shown," Associated Press, March 28, 2004. To see the video, go to http://www.preservemarriage.org.

15. Paulson, "Bishops Try to Mobilize on Marriage."

16. Matthew Rodriguez, "O'Malley Sharpens Attack on Court," *Boston Globe,* February 25, 2004.

17. Catholic Action League, "Catholic Action League Condemns SJC Decision on Same-Sex Marriage," November 18, 2003, http://www.frmcgivney assembly.org/catholicactionleague.html.

18. Gomes, "Moral Imagination."

19. Leviticus 25:44–46 (New Living Testament).

20. John Shelby Spong, "Homosexuality and the Bible," *BaptistWatch.org,* http://www.baptistwatch.org/content/biblegay.html.

21. Spong, "Homosexuality and the Bible."

22. Union of American Hebrew Congregations, *The Torah: A Modern Commentary* (Philadelphia: Jewish Publication Society, 1981), p. 135.

23. Leviticus 18:22, 20:13.

24. *Oxford Companion to the Bible,* ed. Bruce Metzger and Michael Coogan (Oxford: Oxford University Press, 1993), pp. 288–89 ("same-sex sexual relations [were seen as] transgressions of hierarchical gender boundaries. . . . women's attempt to transcend the passive, subordinate role accorded to them by nature [or] men . . . relinquish[ing] the superordinate, active role . . . and . . . descend[ing] to the level of women").

25. Jeffrey Weiss, "If Other Biblical Bans Ignored, Why Are Gay Unions Taboo?" *Philadelphia Inquirer,* February 15, 2004.

26. Spong, "Homosexuality and the Bible."

27. Leviticus 19:33–34.

28. Spong, "Homosexuality and the Bible."

29. Spong, "Homosexuality and the Bible."

30. Reverend John A. Buehrens, *Understanding the Bible,* (Boston: Beacon Press, 2003), p. 9 (emphasis added).

31. Buehrens, *Understanding the Bible*, p. 9.

32. Jim McDermott, "Codifying 'Biblical Principles' of Marriage," *Congressional Record*, February 25, 2004. Another e-mail, which circulated widely as an "open letter" to right-wing commentator Laura Schlessinger, made similar points. It read:

Dear Dr. Laura:

Thank you for doing so much to educate people regarding God's Law. I have learned a great deal from your show, and try to share that knowledge with as many people as I can. When someone tries to defend the homosexual lifestyle, for example, I simply remind them that Leviticus 18:22 clearly states it to be an abomination . . . End of debate. I do need some advice from you, however, regarding some other elements of God's Laws and how to follow them.

1. Leviticus 25:44 states that I may possess slaves, both male and female, provided they are purchased from neighboring nations. A friend of mine claims that this applies to Mexicans, but not Canadians. Can you clarify? Why can't I own Canadians?

2. I would like to sell my daughter into slavery, as sanctioned in Exodus 21:7. In this day and age, what do you think would be a fair price for her?

3. I know that I am allowed no contact with a woman while she is in her period of menstrual uncleanliness—Leviticus 15:19–24. The problem is how do I tell? I have tried asking, but most women take offense.

4. When I burn a bull on the altar as a sacrifice, I know it creates a pleasing odor for the Lord—Leviticus 1:9. The problem is my neighbors. They claim the odor is not pleasing to them. Should I smite them?

5. I have a neighbor who insists on working on the Sabbath. However, Exodus 35:2 clearly states he should be put to death. Am I morally obligated to kill him myself or should I let the police handle it?

6. A friend of mine feels that even though eating shellfish is an abomination, as read in Leviticus 11:10, it is a lesser abomination than homosexuality. I don't agree. Can you settle this? Are there "degrees" of abomination?

7. Leviticus 21:20 states that I may not approach the altar of God if I have a defect in my sight. I have to admit that I wear reading

glasses. Does my vision have to be 20/20, or is there some wiggle room here?

8. Most of my male friends get their hair trimmed, including the hair around their temples, even though this is expressly forbidden by Leviticus 19:27. How should they die?

9. I know from Leviticus 11:6–8 that touching the skin of a dead pig makes me unclean, but may I still play football if I wear gloves?

10. My uncle has a farm. He violates Leviticus 19:19 by planting two different crops in the same field, as does his wife by wearing garments made of two different kinds of threads (cotton/polyester blend). He also tends to curse and blaspheme a lot. Is it really necessary that we go to all the trouble of getting the whole town together to stone them as required by Leviticus 24:10–16? Couldn't we just burn them to death at a private family affair like we do with people who sleep with their in-laws (Leviticus 20:14)?

I know you have studied these things extensively and thus enjoy considerable expertise in such matters, so I am confident you can help. Thank you again for reminding us that God's word is eternal and unchanging.

33. "Editorial: A Step Back," *Boston Globe,* March 30, 2004, http://www.boston.com/news/globe/editorial_opinion/editorials/articles/2004/03/30/a_step_back/.

34. "Editorial: A Step Back."

35. Abraham Lincoln, "Second Inaugural Address," U.S. Capitol, Washington, D.C., March 4, 1865.

36. Leviticus 25:10 (emphasis added).

SEVEN: WHY NOT USE ANOTHER WORD?

1. John Lewis, "At a Crossroads on Gay Unions," *Boston Globe,* October 25, 2003.

2. "Opinions of the Justices to the Senate," SJC-09163 (Massachusetts Supreme Judicial Court, February 3, 2004).

3. Deb Price, "Gay Couple Joins Exclusive Club of Newlyweds," *Detroit News,* December 22, 2003.

4. Lambda Legal, "Gay Man Can Hold Hospital Accountable for Partner's Death After Routine Surgery Following Manhattan Hit-and-Run, Lambda Legal Says," news release, January 9, 2003, http://www.lambdalegal.org/cgi-bin/iowa/documents/record?record=1183.

5. *Baker v. Vermont*, 744 A.2d 864 (Vermont Supreme Court, 1999).

6. *Baker v. Vermont*.

7. Susan M. Murray, Beth Robinson, L. Tracee Whitley, and Peter F. Zupcofska, "Brief of Amici Curiae," regarding "Opinions of the Justices" (Massachusetts Supreme Judicial Court, 2004).

8. Murray et al., "Brief of Amici Curiae."

9. Murray et al., "Brief of Amici Curiae."

10. "Braun: 'Is This Still the Land of Opportunity?' " interview, *USAToday.com,* November 24, 2003, http://www.usatoday.com/news/opinion/editorials/2003-11-23-braun_x.htm.

11. William Safire, "On Same-Sex Marriage," *New York Times,* December 1, 2003, p. A23.

12. Murray et al., "Brief of Amici Curiae."

13. Martin Luther King Jr., *Why We Can't Wait* (New York: Harper & Row, 1964), p. 119.

14. King expressed "grave" disappointment with the "moderate" who "paternalistically believes he can set the timetable for another man's freedom . . . and who constantly advises the Negro to wait for a 'more convenient season.' Shallow understanding from people of good will is much more frustrating than absolute misunderstanding. Lukewarm acceptance is much more bewildering than outright rejection" (*Why We Can't Wait,* pp. 84–85).

15. King, *Why We Can't Wait,* p. 127.

16. Pamela Ferdinand, "Will Vermont Say 'I Do' to Gays?" *Washington Post,* November 19, 1998, p. A2.

17. Mick Meehan, "Historic Presidential Forum at HRC," *Gay City News,* July 18, 2003.

18. *Goodridge v. Department of Public Health,* 440 Mass. 309 (Massachusetts Supreme Judicial Court, 2003).

19. *Goodridge v. Department of Public Health.*

20. "Opinions of the Justices to the Senate."

21. "Opinions of the Justices to the Senate."

22. "The Gubernatorial Debates," *Boston Globe,* October 2, 2002, p. B5.

23. Raphael Lewis and Frank Phillips, "The Gay Marriage Ruling Spotlight on the Governor," *Boston Globe,* November 20, 2003, p. A1.

24. Ellen Goodman, "Gay Unions: Moderation is Winning," *Washington Post,* February 14, 2004, p. A29.

25. Margaret Porter, "State of the States: Vermont Helps Mass. Marriage, While a Partial Victory Is Won in New Jersey," *Out in the Mountains,* February 2004, http://www.mountainpridemedia.org/oitm/issues/2004/02feb2004/fea02_state.htm.

26. Lisa Leff, "Son of Gay Marriage Opponent Marries in San Francisco," March 9, 2004, http://www.mercurynews.com/mld/mercurynews/news/local/states/california/northern_california/8145192.htm.

EIGHT: WILL MARRIAGES IN ONE STATE BE HONORED IN OTHERS?

1. *Estin v. Estin,* 33 U.S. 541, 553 (U.S. Supreme Court, 1943) (Jackson, J., dissenting).

2. Rona Marech, "When the Wedding Bells Stop Ringing," *San Francisco Chronicle,* March 27, 2004.

3. See, e.g., Andrew Koppelman, *The Gay Rights Question in Contemporary American Law* (Chicago: University of Chicago Press, 2002): "In every case that did not involve cohabitation within the forum, and in some that did, Southern courts recognized interracial marriages" (p. 100).

4. Freedom to Marry, "Advice to Couples Planning Marriage in Canada, Massachusetts, and Beyond . . . ," February 4, 2004, http://www.freedomtomarry.org/document.asp?doc_id=1117.

5. Lambda Legal, "We Got Married in Canada, What's Next?" January 1, 2004, http://www.lambdalegal.org/cgi-bin/iowa/documents/record?record=1412.

NINE: IS MARRIAGE EQUALITY A QUESTION
OF CIVIL RIGHTS?

1. Coretta Scott King quoted in International Gay and Lesbian Association, "Coretta Scott King Urges No Vote on Prop. 22," news release, February 29, 2000.

2. On June 24, 2001, Gloria Steinem sent the following statement to the organizers of a rally in support of committed same-sex couples and the freedom to marry:

> If I had married when I was supposed to, I would have lost my name, my legal residence, my credit rating, my ability to get a loan or start a business without my husband's permission—most of my civil rights.
>
> It's taken almost four decades of work by the women's movement to make an equal marriage possible, a parallel to the struggle of suffragists to change marriage laws that turned wives into property, and became the legal model for slavery. Suffragists won a legal identity. Feminists won a legal equality.
>
> But both eras supposed that marriage was about reproduction, that the body of a woman was the means of reproduction and had to be owned by a man. It's a bias that remains with us in the law's refusal to allow two women or two men to marry, no matter how deep and long-lasting their commitment, *yet allows* a heterosexual marriage, no matter how violent or brief its duration. It's a bias that we all have a stake in ending if marriage is to become a true partnership, with or without children, one that says: We love each other. We want to be responsible for each other. We choose to be a family.
>
> I have always supported same-sex marriage, but in retrospect, I think I didn't fully understand the desire to say not just "we are living together," or "we love each other," but, "we are responsible for each other."
>
> Now I do. I pledge myself to work that much harder to make marriage a democratic institution open to everyone, whether or not there are children, a chosen partnership. Marriage is not a privilege. It's a right. Isn't this the country that promised "life, liberty, and the pursuit of happiness?" (http://www.theweddingparty.org/stories/default.html)

3. Karen Breslau and Brad Stone, "Outlaw Vows," *Newsweek*, March 1, 2004, p. 40.

4. Jordan Carleo-Evangelist, "New Paltz Mayor Pleads Not Guilty for Ceremonies," *Albany (N.Y.) Times Union*, March 4, 2004, p. A1.

5. Claudia Rowe, "Brides and Joy—a Long Love Story," *Seattle Post-Intelligencer*, March 4, 2004, p. A11.

6. Marcella Bombardieri, "Jackson Wary of Same-Sex Rift," *Boston Globe*, February 17, 2004, p. B1.

7. *Boston Globe* staff, "The Constitutional Convention: Impassioned Arguments/Oratory," *Boston Globe*, February 12, 2004, p. B8.

8. "After the Convention/Blocking a Vote," *Boston Globe*, February 14, 2004, p. B5.

9. Coretta Scott King, speech given at Lambda Legal Defense and Education Fund luncheon, March 31, 1998.

10. John Lewis, speech given at Fortieth Anniversary Civil Rights March, Washington, D.C., August 23, 2003.

11. Eric Deggans, "Similar Struggles? Gay Rights and Civil Rights," *St. Petersburg Times*, January 18, 2004, p. 1P.

12. Debra J. Saunders, "Rosa Parks—Not," *San Francisco Chronicle*, February 23, 2004, p. B7.

13. Jennifer Peter, "Gay Rights Debate Gets Civil Rights Feel," *Boston Globe*, January 15, 2004.

14. Rick Klein, "Gridlock in Marriage Debate," *Boston Globe*, February 13, 2004, p. A1

15. *365Gay.com* staff, "MLK Widow Condemns Anti-Gay Amendment," March 24, 2004, http://www.365gay.com/newscon04/03/032404KingMarry.htm.

16. Lynette Clementson, "Both Sides Court Black Churches in the Battle Over Gay Marriage," *New York Times*, March 1, 2004, p. A1.

17. John Lewis, *Walking with the Wind* (New York: Simon & Schuster, 1998).

18. The National Black Justice Coalition Web site is www.nbjcoalition.org.

19. See Evan Wolfson, "Civil Rights, Human Rights, Gay Rights: Minorities and the Humanity of the Different," *Harvard Journal of Law and Public Policy* 14 (1991): 22.

20. Keith Boykin, *One More River to Cross: Black & Gay in America* (New York: Anchor, 1996); see also www.nbjcoalition.org.

21. La Opinión, "Es Una Cuestión de Derechos," February 21, 2004, http://www.laopinion.com/editorial/?rkey=00040220182721372275.

22. Henry Louis Gates Jr., "Blacklash?" *New Yorker*, May 17, 1993.

23. Gates, "Blacklash?" pp. 42–43.

24. *Federalist* 10.

25. *Federalist* 51.

26. *Whitney v. California*, 274 U.S. 357, 375 (U.S. Supreme Court, 1927) (Brandeis, J., concurring).

27. *Federalist* 78.

28. Gates, "Blacklash?" p. 43.

29. Martin Lutrell, "Foes of Same-Sex Marriage Rally," *Worcester Telegram & Gazette*, January 26, 2004, p. A1.

30. David Moats, "Freedom-to-Marry Activists Borrow Strategy from Fight for Racial Equality," *San Jose Mercury News*, February 22, 2004, p. 1.

31. Gates, "Blacklash?" p. 43.

32. Eric Deggans, "Gay Rights/Civil Rights," *St. Petersburg Times Online*, January 18, 2004, http://www.sptimes.com/2004/01/18/Columns/Gay_rights civil_rights.shtml.

33. Evan Wolfson, "Crossing the Threshold: Equal Marriage Rights for Lesbians and Gay Men, and the Intra-Community Critique," *New York University Review of Law & Social Change* 21 (1994): 586 ("We lesbians and gay men are a 'remarkably diverse group' . . . not always visible, even to those lesbians and gay men who are the most visible").

34. Lewis, *Walking with the Wind*, p. 273.

35. Drew Hansen, *The Dream: Martin Luther King, Jr. and the Speech that Inspired a Nation* (New York: Ecco, 2003).

36. Hansen, *The Dream*.

37. Hansen, *The Dream*, p. 12.

38. Hansen, *The Dream*, pp. 164–65. Hansen correctly observes that change did not happen overnight. "But on August 28, 1963, King began the long-overdue process of changing America's idea of itself. He gave the nation a vocabulary to express what was happening in the civil rights revolution . . . This transformation in America's self-conception has happened only over many

years, as King's speech at the march has slowly remade the American imagination" (p. 227).

39. Martin Luther King Jr., *Why We Can't Wait,* (New York: Harper & Row, 1964), pp. 80–81.

40. Ibid. at 86.

TEN: WHY THE FREEDOM TO MARRY MATTERS TO ME

1. Martin Luther King Jr., *Why We Can't Wait,* (New York: Harper & Row, 1964), p. 152.

APPENDIX A: BIG QUESTIONS, SHORT ANSWERS

1. These short answers to key questions, or talking points, draw on materials originally prepared by the Marriage Project at Lambda Legal Defense & Education Fund with helpful suggestions from many around the country.

APPENDIX B: DISCRIMINATION: PROTECTIONS DENIED TO SAME-SEX COUPLES AND THEIR KIDS

1. See the report at http://www.thetaskforce.org/marriagecenter/GAO Benefits.pdf.

2. See, e.g., the excellent materials available through Gay & Lesbian Advocates & Defenders at http://www.glad.org/Publications/CivilRightProject/PBOsOfMarriage.pdf (June 2001).

APPENDIX C: GETTING INVOLVED

1. Martin Luther King Jr., *Why We Can't Wait* (New York: Harper & Row, 1964), p. 34.

2. Chris Taylor, "I Do . . . No, You Don't!" *Time,* March 1, 2004.

3. Dan Kennedy, "Safe for Now," *Boston Phoenix,* February 13, 2004.

4. Yvonne Abraham, "Debate Humanized Issue, Legislators," *Boston Globe,* February 15, 2004.

5. Rick Klein, "Gridlock in Marriage Debate," *Boston Globe*, February 13, 2004, p. A1.

6. Abraham, "Debate Humanized Issue, Legislators," *Boston Globe*, February 15, 2004.

7. Kristin Lombardi, "Then There Were Three," *Boston Phoenix*, February 27, 2004.

8. President John F. Kennedy, The White House, Washington, D.C., June 11, 1963.

INDEX